*Vocation and Identity
in the Fiction of
Muriel Spark*

Vocation and Identity
in the Fiction of
Muriel Spark

Rodney Stenning Edgecombe

University of Missouri Press
Columbia and London

Copyright © 1990 by
The Curators of the University of Missouri
University of Missouri Press, Columbia, Missouri 65201
Printed and bound in the United States of America
All rights reserved
5   4   3   2   1   94   93   92   91   90

Library of Congress Cataloging-in-Publication Data

Edgecombe, Rodney Stenning.
   Vocation and identity in the fiction of Muriel Spark / Rodney
Stenning Edgecombe.
      p.   cm.
   Includes bibliographical references and index.
   ISBN 0–8262–0750–2 (alk. paper)
   1. Spark, Muriel—Criticism and interpretation.   2. Identity
(Psychology) in literature.   3. Vocation in literature.   I. Title.
PR6037.P29Z64   1990
823'.914—dc20   90–40537
                                                            CIP

∞™ This paper meets the requirements of the
American National Standard for Permanence of Paper
for Printed Library Materials, Z39.48, 1984.

Designer: Liz Fett
Typesetter: Connell-Zeko Type & Graphics
Printer: Thomson-Shore, Inc.
Binder: Thomson-Shore, Inc.
Type face: Melliza

For my mother, Lilian Ruth Edgecombe;
and in memory of my brother,
Terence Stenning Edgecombe

Contents

Acknowledgments

The quotations from *The Bachelors* (copyright © 1960 by Muriel Spark), *The Girls of Slender Means* (copyright © 1963 by Muriel Spark), *The Mandelbaum Gate* (copyright © 1965 by Muriel Spark), *The Abbess of Crewe* (copyright © 1974 by Verwaltungs A. G.), and *The Takeover* (copyright © 1976 by Verwaltungs A. G.) by permission of the publishers Macmillan, and of the author's agents David Higham Associates Ltd.

I should like to thank the librarians of Jagger Library, University of Cape Town, especially the staff of the Inter-Library Loans Department, as well as Father Donald de Beer of St. Mary's Cathedral, Cape Town, and Father Bonaventure Hinwood, OFM, of the St. John-Baptist Vianney Seminary, Pretoria, for clarifying aspects of Catholicism for me. Any Protestant errors remaining in the text must be laid squarely at my door, however. I am above all especially grateful to the Research Committee of the University of Cape Town for a grant which covered all my expenses.

*Vocation and Identity
in the Fiction of
Muriel Spark*

. . . she had a meaning, even if she had no meaningful intention.

—*The Girls of Slender Means*

Introduction

Muriel Spark's first novel is not, like many others, a tentative trial of form, or a cautious, exploratory testing of the voice. Rather, it is a supremely confident piece of work that anticipates many of the themes and techniques of her maturity. Its Minerva-like sufficiency can be attributed perhaps to its relatively late arrival in the creative life of its author, who had devoted her energies to belles lettres and poetry before trying her hand at fiction. As Ruth Whittaker has noted, Spark "was initially reluctant to commit herself to a genre so apparently formless in comparison with her earlier discipline as a poet."[1] Moreover, it has become a commonplace of Spark criticism to relate the finding of her novelistic voice to her Catholic conversion, the one vocation being seen to issue in the other. She herself has laid the foundation for this line of thought in her manifesto "My Conversion": "I think there is a connection between my writing and my conversion but I don't want to be too dogmatic about it."[2] I propose, then, to look at the way in which the idea of vocation, whether it be construed in a literally religious or in an extended, secular sense, provides Spark with a recurring center of interest and thematic resource. While it is in terms of this topic that I shall focus the matter of the novels, I shall at the same time address the distinctive nature of the voice that was found (as if by a ventrilo-quial extension of the *vox* in "vocation") in her conversion. In this regard, I shall argue that the fiction can best be handled in the generic context of epigram.

The novelist's apprenticeship as a poet, if not unique, is certainly unusual, and it is probably responsible for the combination of finiteness and elusiveness that characterizes her work. Frank Bal-

---

1. *The Faith and Fiction of Muriel Spark*, 127.
2. W. J. Weatherby, "Muriel Spark: My Conversion," 59.

danza, for example, commenting on the precocious maturity of *The Comforters*, has noted that "its greatest virtue is that it holds in suspension a huge variety of possibilities for the aesthetic exploitation of meanings."[3] In the idea of suspension we have a key to a central feature of Spark's work: its concern not with comprehensiveness and encompassing statement, but with an obliquity that is content to polish and facet a part of the truth at any one time, since it knows its necessary limitation cannot enfold the whole. The novels, as I hope to show, are best viewed as *expanded* epigrams, with all the specious finality or, conversely, the elegant incompleteness that characterizes the form. What is left out of the epigram (where a pattern of verbal balance necessarily exscinds everything the pattern cannot contain) is allowed to float around it as a nimbus of additional meaning, suspended because suggested, without being given final form. Epigrams, in a word, are verbal icebergs, and Spark's novels show similarly shapely, glacial peaks above masses of submerged implication. Phyllis Grosskurth, in an interesting (but in my view mistaken) account of the early novels, has correlated length with high seriousness. She suggests that in the works preceding *The Mandelbaum Gate,* the narrow compass justifies the "sudden capricious juxtaposition of moving from one element of reality to another; . . . the few telling details of caricature; and the loose ends and detached scenes," all of which features she then dismisses as "short-cuts" that "won't do in a full-scale novel."[4] If "short-cuts" are meant to signify evasions of artistic duty, the charge is unjust. In Spark's work, things *are* cut short, but rather in the time-honored way of ellipsis, where the termination is heavy with the unspoken meanings lying beyond the track of the three full stops. In epigram, if not in "full-scale" novels, there is implicit acknowledgment of the fact that this is an enriching rather than an impoverishing procedure. And it is worth readjusting our categories as a means of reaching a fairer assessment of the writer.

The comparatively restricted scope of Spark's novels has allowed her to be immensely productive, and for the purposes of this study I shall select only five of the eighteen she has so far written. My choice is far from random. By now the shape of Spark's career has become apparent, and three clearly marked phases can be seen to inform it. The first centers largely on documenting the concerns of tight-knit British communities, whether it be the literary Bohe-

3. "Muriel Spark and the Occult," 196.
4. "The World of Muriel Spark: Spirits or Spooks?" 66.

mia of London in the fifties, or a group of Scots schoolgirls two decades before that, or life in a working-class suburb. Critical consensus regards this as her best phase, including as it does *The Comforters* (1957), *Memento Mori* (1959), and *The Prime of Miss Jean Brodie* (1961). To represent this early period I have chosen two novels, *The Bachelors* (1960) and *The Girls of Slender Means* (1963), because I regard these as being as much worthy of critical acclaim as the masterpieces (more exhaustively treated) that flank them. After the run of British novels, *The Mandelbaum Gate* was published in 1965. Its personal cast and uncharacteristic length marked a break with the manner of the earlier fiction, though hindsight enables one to link it with later pieces such as *Loitering with Intent*. I include it here not only on the strength of its merits (which I believe to be considerable) but also because it is so much a novel sui generis. *The Mandelbaum Gate* is followed by an "exilic" era, the time of Spark's residence abroad. As Velma Richmond has pointed out, the novels from this period are marked by a "darkening vision,"[5] a vision which only partly accounts for the unpleasant quality some of them reveal. The material is sometimes so attenuated as to seem sapless and summary, epigrams that have collapsed in upon themselves for want of paradoxical tension. Although Ruth Whittaker has attempted a sympathetic study of these works in her outstanding book on Spark, she is still forced to concede that they "invite comparison with the hard, impersonal quality of the *nouveau roman*."[6] I am not much attracted by this period, which stretches from *The Public Image* (1968) to *The Abbess of Crewe* (1974), and shall look only at the last, a masterpiece in which Spark's thinning of her matter (something which renders, say, *The Public Image* so insubstantial) is justified by the airiness of its mock-heroic mode.

The novels from *The Takeover* (1976) onward seem to offer a synthesis of the preceding phases, two set in rich continental society, two reverting to the postwar austerities of London, and all of them to a greater or lesser degree enyclopedic rather than aphoristic (though *The Only Problem* has a chill, spare texture reminiscent of the seventies). In my view they mark an advance on the heartless economy of the intermediate fiction, but fail to match the achievement of the early works.

Before I turn to the minutiae of form and texture, and the themes

5. "The Darkening Vision of Muriel Spark."
6. *Faith and Fiction*, 1.

of vocation and identity they support, I need to defend the claim that Spark's novels are best viewed as extended epigrams. An epigram that outgrows a succinct sentence in many respects forfeits its claim to the title, and when it inflates to the size even of Spark's most compact novellas, the term can be applied only in a metaphoric way. Joseph Hynes has set her work against the concerns of conventional realists and has suggested that her "reality principle . . . is summed up in Blake's language [To see a World in a Grain of Sand / And a Heaven in a Wild Flower / Hold Infinity in the palm of your hand / And Eternity in an hour]."[7] *Multum in parvo* has never been high on the novel's agenda, however, and from its birth it has shown signs of gigantism. It is in this context then, the context of *War and Peace* and the Victorian triple-decker, that Spark's novels take on an epigrammatic status, showing within their restricted limits some of the distinctive features of the kind.

What are those features? Distillation, suppression of all matter which threatens perfection of form, and a preference for partial to total truth are some. This would partly account for Malcolm Bradbury's diagnosis—"From [Spark's] works the beginning, which creates expectation and freedom, and the middle, which substantiates and qualifies it, have gone. Her characters arise at the last, and *from* the last; and what has withered away is substantially a world of motive and purpose and aspiration."[8] Likewise arising at the last and from the last, epigrams aspire to being impersonal, even inscrutable. Although they can be highly tendentious, they pass themselves off as considered wisdom, dispassionately extracted from, rather than imposed upon, experience at large. This much is evident at the very dawn of the form. In the *Oxford Classical Dictionary* Gilbert Highet describes the epigrams of Simonides as having a "grave intensity of feeling . . . enhanced by their brevity and impersonality."[9] The unemotive spareness of the Christian creeds and catechisms, by virtue of similar qualities, might also be said to bear an epigrammatic relation to the body of dogma they represent, and they are quoted by Spark at crucial nodes of her stories to bring the contingent detail of the narrative into the focus of the divine "epigrams" that underpin them.

The pithiness of epigram underwrites its emotional restraint. Feeling cannot burgeon if it is not allowed the space to do so, and

7. *The Art of the Real: Muriel Spark's Novels*, 35.
8. "Muriel Spark's Fingernails," 246.
9. "Epigram," *Oxford Classical Dictionary*, 392. Henceforth cited parenthetically in the text by page number.

the feeling that has obviously been excluded is the more potent for being felt as a pressure against the frame keeping it at bay. Josephine Jacobsen has said of Spark that she "effects what she effects by her style, which is less a literary technique than, itself, her own instrument of transfiguration. By elision, by focus, by a buried explosion, she pursues her interest—that of explaining permanent scale and proportion by the telling of a story in her own style."[10] The epigram was born in the matrix of the epitaph, and succinctness and restraint in circumstances that would more conventionally have called for emotional largesse are among its properties—to quote Gilbert Highet again, "the archaic epigram was a brief address in which a tombstone or votive tablet (or sometimes the dead man) spoke to the passer-by, giving him the necessary facts with strongly restrained emotion. This control and purpose made the epigram into an art-form" (p. 392).

A necessary adjunct of "control" and "impersonality" is neatness—pattern that unflinchingly tidies up the rough edges of life that menace its containing powers. Successful epigrams seem indeed to demand a sense of *sprezzatura*, the *effortless* encompassment of experience in all its thorniness and intractability. The Roman epigrammatist Martial is a case in point, for, as J. W. Duff has observed, "he writes with a finished neatness of expression and a freshness that reads like improvisation," though Duff concedes that the contemplative distance that epigram requires can issue in "too heartless an indifference,"[11] a charge that Spark's detractors have made again and again. There *are* occasions when a reverence for pattern, advanced at the expense of human "mess," can produce a clinical dispatch and perfunctoriness in the novelist's procedures, and I have already made clear my dissatisfaction with those middle-period works which do precisely that. However, at its most potent, which is to say its most appropriate, the novel-cum-epigram can manage to fuse elegance and intensity in the best tradition of the form. La Rochefoucauld's *maximes* are verbal concentrates, boiled down to their essence from "dilute" statements, but owing their truth to the thoughts that have evaporated along the way. I hope to show that something similar holds true for Spark. As long as her Catholicism is present in the background of her fiction, it provides ballast and weight for her epigrammatic procedure. But when, as in the middle-period fiction, it is underplayed, all the attendant dan-

---

10. "A Catholic Quartet," 142.
11. *A Literary History of Rome in the Silver Age*, 409.

gers of that method—triviality, heartlessness, flatness—start to exert their unpleasant influence. Samuel Hynes has noted that if Spark "is detached in her attitude toward her characters, this is understandable in a novelist who sees people in terms of the designs into which they fit (including the design of the Four Last Things)."[12] I shall argue, indeed, that those designs are essential for the success of some of the early novels, and that the Catholicism that suffuses them, far from impairing their universality, actually gives them substance.

12. "The Prime of Muriel Spark," 563, 567.

1

The Bachelors

Secular Vocation

Whereas the realistic novel has always tried to encompass its material, the epigram has been content to contain. That is to say, its effort has centered less on getting than on got, on formulation rather than on the full substance of what is being formulated. In epigrams we are constantly aware of the capsular shell of words that brackets and holds a perception. This capsularity—in an extended form—can be detected in the overarching structure of *The Bachelors*, where it is evident in the beginning and the end of the novel.

At the start, London, with a sweeping appositive, is termed a "city of bachelors"—an epigrammatic offering of a half-truth for a whole: "Daylight was appearing over London, the great city of bachelors. Half-pint bottles of milk began to be stood on the doorsteps of houses containing single apartments from Hampstead Heath to Greenwich Park . . . ."[1] At the end, this restrictive epithet is displaced by one more ample in its reference ("metropolitan"), which opens up the perspective at the very moment that it screws home the chiastic brace:

> He walked round the houses, calculating, to test his memory, the
> numbers of the bachelors—thirty-eight thousand five hundred streets,
> and seventeen point one bachelors to a street—lying awake, twisting
> and murmuring, or agitated with their bedfellows, or breathing in
> deep repose between their sheets, all over London, the metropolitan
> city. (p. 241)

The epigrammatic flavor of the start and finish is not limited only to the enclosing design, but can be detected also in the impersonal

---

1. Spark, *The Bachelors*, 1. Hereafter cited parenthetically in the text by page number.

tone so often associated with epigram. So it is that the metonymic milk bottles are put out in the passive rather than the active voice, and the focus is directed away from perceiver to the perception itself. This sterilizing dissociation of the voice from its utterance also registers in the statistics that end the novel, which comically (but maimingly) convert human beings into decimal points. Ronald's consciousness relays these numbers as a memory exercise on one level, but the author's voice is also to some extent present, fading out its immediate concern with character and event into a cold world of figures. The movement from Ronald's to the narrator's presence is almost seamless, and it is only when the phrasal duplication of "city of bachelors" in "metropolitan city" occurs that we become aware that the novel has finally been encased in its sheath of epigram. The antiphony of morning and night also enhances the sense of balance and brings to mind the demarcating interludes in *The Waves*.

The opening of *The Bachelors*, incidentally, also owes something to eighteenth-century genre poems of awakening and *levée*. Pope's description of Belinda's bedroom in *The Rape of the Lock* refers collectively to sleepless lovers, and Swift's "A Description of the Morning" also deals with stereotypic figures going about their daily ritual. At a later stage of her career Spark will have no qualms about writing whole novels in the present tense, but here she avoids the frequentative verbs with which Swift and Pope evoke a sense of habit. Instead she uses the narrative preterit, jarring it with subjunctives of prediction: "In Queen's Gate, . . . and in King's Road, Chelsea, the bachelors stirred between their sheets, . . . then, remembering it was Saturday morning, turned over on their pillows. But soon, since it was Saturday, most would be out on the streets . . ." (p. 1). Spark then goes on to describe how they set out in droves at a particular time in order to avoid contact with the "rightful" shoppers, the women with families to tend and feed. Her stress on the collective habits of the bachelors is designed to present the community in rather more monolithic terms than it actually warrants, so as to create a "unifying background," comparable with the backgrounds of age in *Memento Mori*, of the school in *The Prime of Miss Jean Brodie*, and of the hostel in *The Girls of Slender Means*. Her generality, reductive and therefore mechanizing, bears comparison with the generalizing bent of epigram, which also makes data fit a pattern, conscious that the fit is a Procrustean one. It is important for her purposes in this novel that bachelorhood should be associated with guilt and that the characters should regard their status as a stigma. The collective way in which their behavior is described is thus also meant to give it a subcultural pattern, a kind of cautious and apologetic freemasonry. Once she has established her background in the compass of a mere page, Spark inserts some characteristic dialogue to foreground two of her protagonists.

The high proportion of dialogue to discursive commentary is yet another feature of Spark's fiction, one that links it to the novels of Ivy Compton-Burnett. Like the latter's, her account of circumstances surrounding her characters is often in the nature of a playwright's directives or, since single details are sometimes made to tell in a luminous way, of the lyric. This, perhaps, is also a legacy of her poetic apprenticeship to story-writing. It is in the exchange and dialectic of voices that Spark chooses to advance her plots. The conversation below is so banal as to suggest oneness with the "vocational" shoppers the bachelors have taken pains to avoid—the bachelors, for all their "otherness," are as much subject to inflation and the vagaries of the balance of payments as anyone else in the supermarkets. Matter, as Spark terms the material universe, cannot be evaded by anyone, most especially by anyone who shops:

> "Clayton's."
> "How much?"
> "One and six. That's for a small packet; does for two. A large one is two and six; six helpings."
> "Terrible price," said Ronald agreeably.
> "Your hand's never out of your pocket," said Martin. (p. 2)

This deadpan enumeration of prices, its flatness flattened further by the ellipsis that draws attention to the information away from the style, is recalled a page or so later when Ronald repeats Martin's formula. Such repetition, while it seems to be an automated response in keeping with the mechanical, Bergsonian treatment of the bachelors, also shows that Ronald conforms to everyday rituals out of kindness to his friends, however aware of their banality he might be. If we have been alert enough, we will thus have learned something of his character even before the author begins to describe it, proof enough of her economy. Spark's repetition is therefore at once comic, structural, and commentative. And it is immediately explained. A narrative flashback allows us to see that Ronald has had to work hard at achieving his kindly tolerance. Through it we also arrive at an exposition of the novel's overriding concern—the nature and scope of vocation: "'No,' the American specialist had said, irritable with the strain of putting a technical point into common speech, 'there is no reason why your intellect should be impaired except, of course, that you cannot exercise it to the full extent that would be possible were you able to follow and rise to the top of a normal career'" (p. 5).

Ronald's disability, his epileptic fits, is one to which he must gradually become reconciled, and one which he must somehow integrate into his life in order to make meaningful—hence his desire to remain conscious during his seizures. In this respect he resembles the Job figures who occur throughout Spark's fiction, figures who, like Pia de Donati in *The Divine Comedy*, have achieved serenity by conforming their wills to the greater will of God. In the words of J. H. Dorenkamp, a Spark character who "would act prudentially must first adopt God's point of view and then conform his own actions to that view."[2] One of the most moving of these "conformists" is Jean Taylor in *Memento Mori*, whose achievement in doing so is linked to the *Magnificat* (the Virgin Mary's response to the Incarnation): "Jean Taylor lingered for a time, employing her pain to magnify the Lord, and meditating sometimes confidingly upon Death, the first of the four last things ever to be remembered."[3]

Ronald's response is of a different order, but it is as hard earned. He is at first embittered at being denied various opportunities by his epilepsy:

"A vocation to the priesthood is the will of God. Nothing can change God's will. You are an epileptic. No epileptic can be a priest. Ergo you never had a vocation. But you can do something else."

"I could never be first-rate."

"That is sheer vanity"—it was an old priest speaking—"you were never meant to be a first-rate careerist."

"Only a first-rate epileptic?"

"Indeed, yes. Quite seriously, yes," the old priest said. (p. 7)

Human aspirations at odds with the providential design have obviously to be surrendered; pride has to be tempered. Spark's identification of the interlocutor at the word *vanity* makes the "old priest" resemble the preacher in Ecclesiastes, so that vanity comes to signify not only the self-absorption that is the source of Ronald's despair at this point in his life, but also the vanity, the nullity, that issues from disregarding the will of God.

The desire to excel at all costs registers also in the monomaniac way in which the word *first-rate* keeps recurring in Ronald's thoughts,

2. "Moral Vision in Muriel Spark's *The Prime of Miss Jean Brodie*," 6.
3. Spark, *Memento Mori*, 246.

so that even the nurse at the clinic to which he has gone to cure his disorder strikes him as being so. Like George Herbert in "Affliction (I)," he has made fineness a *finis*, an end in itself. Disappointment at not being able to excel in his own right makes him petulant, but in one of his bouts of bad temper he comes to a self-realization that might almost be termed an anagnorisis. He feels within himself the "potentialities of a most unpleasant young man" (p. 8).

Potentialities can either be realized or betrayed, as Spark herself has observed in an interview with Ian Gillham: "There were teachers at my school who had these potentialities within themselves—perhaps they didn't even know it but they must have betrayed it. And completely unrealised potentialities—that's what Jean Brodie represents."[4] The potentialities here are synonymous with the biblical talents which "it is death to hide," but human beings, according to the Catholic economy so firmly endorsed by Ronald himself, are prone to sin, and salvation depends as much on the exorcism of negative potentialities as on the realization of the positive. That Ronald decides to submit to, rather than to resist, the divine will, can be measured by his cheerful self-quotation (all passion spent) shortly after the encounter with the nurse: "I'll be a first-rate epileptic and that will be my career" (p. 8). The doctor's response in this "divine" humor is secular and grim, however, for he is irritated at having to admit his impotence to solve the problem of pain. All he can do is document his patient's incurable disorder in that medical analogue of the *liber scriptus*, the card index. Ronald's facetiousness is not bitter, but rather the result of new-won peace of mind. A comparably sanctified impudence, one might remark in passing, is found in the words attributed to St. Lawrence during his martyrdom on a gridiron—"Turn me over, for I am done on this side."

Ronald accommodates his disability by confronting it, whereas another doctor insists on medical euphemism, as if the epilepsy were somehow made manageable by the jargon of his profession. When Ronald talks cheerfully and honestly of "fits," the doctor hushes him with "seizure." Ronald's serenity, born of self-acceptance, also enables him to deal with his father's distress at the notion of having a disabled son. Spark's irony turns on the fact that it is the "disabled" one who takes the initiative in organizing a life for his father, otherwise terrified of the encumbrance. In the spare narrative that presents this episode, the father smiles (p. 11) and, as so often in the novel, the detail, without any authorial pointers,

4. "Keeping It Short," 411.

takes on a cryptic inscrutability. We are left puzzling the nature of the smile—is it simply relaxed gratitude, or is it incredulity at the son's firmness and command of circumstance, qualities so much at odds with the idea of "incurability"? Spark's gnomic method is not without its Sphinxian moments.

Like his father, Ronald's girlfriend Hildegarde also fails to accept the strength his self-knowledge confers, so he ends the affair and embraces a life of celibacy. This chasteness becomes part of his vocation, since it is closely bound up with his epilepsy. Vocation need not necessarily have a priestly implication; it can also be taken to refer to any sense of a calling secured by submission to the will of God, and by the faithful conviction that there is a pattern in terms of which life can take on meaning. So patronage, especially a patronage that, relying on the clichés of pregnancy ("eating for two"), reduces a strong adult to a condition of infantility, has to be discarded: "'You have a better memory than mine,' Ronald said one Sunday morning when they were slopping about in their bedroom slippers in Ronald's room. 'I shall be able to memorise for both of us,' she said" (p. 14). The same response is repeated later, and, as so often, it becomes an incremental refrain. Instead of the innocuous, mechanical *memorise*, Hildegarde uses *remember* (p. 14), a verb much more insidiously vicarious and much more likely to violate the privacy of Ronald's being.

The more poignantly to indicate the isolation of his life since giving up the affair, Spark now follows him into a public house frequented by other bachelor friends. These she introduces in a compressed epic "list," sketching details as briskly as possible. At the start of the novel, she generated her humor along Bergsonian lines, mechanizing the bachelors as a collective, marching them out to shop at a set time, and having them live their lives in an unnatural unison. Here, by contrast, she strikes a note of disparateness and incompatibility. Some kind of community *is* conferred, but only in retrospect, and in a way that subverts the predictable phrase "confirmed bachelor" by another suggesting the graded membership of a religious order. Here is a faint pre-echo of the travestied vocations she will come more and more to foreground in her later fiction. The impression of contingency extends through the dialogue that follows, the source of which could be some Absurdist play, so disconnected and cross-purposed and solipsistic is its effect:

> "Nice to see you all together," Ronald said.
> "Eggs, boiled and poached only," Walter Prett read out in a sad voice from his diet sheet. . . .

"I've got mounds of homework," said Ewart Thornton, "because the half-term tests have begun."
Matthew went over to the bar and brought back two pickled onions on a plate, and ate them. (p. 16)

Ronald's greeting salutes what seems to be a community, but which the description has already shown to be a herd of individuals hardly conscious of each other. The pub scene could have been more fully documented, interconnections could have been made, and thematic inferences drawn, but Spark prefers to touch in the picture here and there with dabs of narrative detail, allowing the sense of disjunctiveness to take full effect. She withholds information that will later explain some of the apparently inconsequential details: Walter Prett is overweight, hence the dramatic modulations as he reads his diet list, made over by his passionate *sforzandi* into an elegy for sacrificed food; Matthew Finch eats onions as an (often futile) guarantee of chastity; and Ewart Thornton's prosaic remark—announcements about his schoolwork recur throughout the novel—countervails Walter's theatrical manner, and also indicates an unlovely self-concern. This is the ill-assorted circle of Ronald's acquaintance, a circle that, as in a Venn diagram, overlaps with the additional cast of spiritualists to form the entire dramatis personae of *The Bachelors*. The overlapping is effected by various *ficelles*, as Henry James called his integrating characters. They are Martin Bowles, who will later prosecute the medium Patrick Seton, Thornton, and Ronald himself, who will give evidence at the trial.

It is to spiritualism that Spark turns once she has completed her exposition of the book's nominal subject. The pivotal figure, a medium, is also a bachelor, but his "bachelorhood" has a very different cast from Ronald's. It results rather from his failure to commit himself to human beings, his emotional retardation, and his cult of the immaterial. Spark provides visual indices to these shortcomings when she describes his appearance, juxtaposing silver and yellow in her description of his hair, an odd indeterminateness that invites contrary constructions of youth and age. The mixture of colors, moreover, suggests blond hair in a state of neglect, something picked up also in Seton's gray complexion. While this again summons up an image of dirt, it also associates him with the ectoplasmic apparitions it is his vocation to invoke. In *Loitering with Intent* Spark similarly associates grayness with insubstantiality when the narrator observes: "For the moment I felt like a grey figment, the 'I' of a novel whose physical description the author had decided not to set forth."[5]

Seton's mode of speaking, with a *diminuendo* at the end of each sentence, is yet another pointer to his bloodlessness, for his speech registers as an indistinct, echoic aftermath, much like the medium's own voice in relation to his "control's." And in the seance to which the narrator cuts shortly after this, we are told that threads of ectoplasm fall from his mouth like tape (p. 31), a simile which curiously reverses our sense of the immaterial and the real. For the author the ectoplasm appears to have greater substance than the haberdashery she uses to describe it—a position very different from Browning's in *Mr. Sludge, "the Medium."* Like Ronald, she would seem to find spiritualism a credible set of beliefs, rejecting it only because of its "demonic" origins.

However, the author's belief in what many dismiss as a spurious "religion" in no way softens her satire of its schismatic impulses and banal suburban contexts. Catholicism, especially the preconciliar Catholicism of *The Bachelors,* is nothing if not monolithic, and believers have (sometimes painfully) to conform to an unalterable and objective body of dogma. One legacy of Protestantism, with its stress on inward revelation, has been the spawning of various ad hoc cults (like that of the charismatic paganism satirized in *The Takeover*). By allowing the individual to dissent from established doctrine, it has opened the way to schism. This tendency is apparent also in spiritualism. Marlene, Patrick Seton's patron, has launched various purges in the movement and created sects within sects, the *sanctum sanctorum* of which is the "Interior Spiral." Her modern flat has a room that has been converted by a placard with Gothic lettering into "The Wider Infinity." As if in mockery of this cramped city building, an epigraph from Scripture reads, "In my Father's house are many mansions." The sham antiquarianism of that Gothic script, the cardboard fiat that abolishes a little room and replaces it, Donne style, with an "everywhere," and the cavalier use of Scripture for a purpose it was never meant to serve—these details are meant to alert as much as to entertain the reader. So too the fact that the seance room adjoins Marlene's kitchen, the serving hatch of which gives her access to the other world in the best traditions of Augustan mock-heroic. Her "liturgical" reforms are no less funny and pointed: she has abolished a "hymn" that, dimly recollecting the sacred parodies of secular tunes produced in the Middle Ages,

5. Spark, *Loitering with Intent*, 95.

has grafted a spiritualist text onto "She'll be coming down the mountain when she comes." Yet, although the setting and the circumstances are grotesque, the activities are sinister, and Seton manages to latch on to truths about people that he subsequently uses to blackmail them. In making him so far credible, Spark seems again to be suggesting that the evil he represents is as real as it is horrifying and that, once the Mephistophelian glamour that often masks it has been stripped away, it is as commonplace in suburbia as it is in hell.

Since she is a spokesperson for spiritualism, Marlene's encounter with Ronald dramatizes the opposed values at the center of the novel. She begins by avowing her anti-Catholic prejudices and reminds Ronald, in an extended flashback, of comparable past encounters with hostile Protestants and non-believers. It is clear from this that he has tried to forge his Catholicism to his everyday life. Although his priestly vocation has been thwarted by his epilepsy, it is still incumbent on him to be a *fidei defensor*—the responsibility of apologetics cannot be shirked in the secular society through which he moves. What is striking is the patient gradation of his response to suit the different kinds of rudeness. His answers are mostly kind and controlled. Only once does he walk out, and, when he is forced to be combative, he regrets his uncharity. His adaptability fulfills the Pauline notion of being all things to all people, however wearisome he might find the task. It is a quality hard won, and the recurring situation (the adverb *sometimes* comes again and again as in a parodic litany) hints at the existentialist nausea that besets him throughout the novel. As we move out of the flashback into the present clash with Marlene, the narrator suggests by adverbs of habit that it is actually as stale and predictable as all those that have just been replayed. Clearly, moreover, the catalog of responses is drawn from her own experience, and seems to offer itself to the reader as a detachable pamphlet: "How to deal with Anti-Catholic Prejudice: The Socratic Method." Such pragmatism is a feature of many Spark novels, but it reaches a peak in *A Far Cry from Kensington,* where the narrator sets so much store by her advice that she generously waives payment: "I offer this advice without fee; it is included in the price of this book."[6] Being a Catholic in a secular society demands a degree of grit, even heroism. While it certainly consoles and directs him, Ronald's faith also exposes him to discomfort. Irving Malin has noted in this respect that "Catholicism

6. Spark, *A Far Cry from Kensington,* 11.

for Mrs Spark . . . emerges as a 'rock' from which the reader can survey the human condition."[7] That is true, and it is true also for many of her characters, Ronald among them. What it does not take into account, however, is that rocks are exposed and windy places, and quite as discomfiting to inhabit as the oceans they survey.

Whatever the biographical background that has gone into its fictional presentation, Ronald's encounter with Marlene shows him to have integrated religion and living. His tough integrity also lies behind an outburst to Matthew Finch later in the novel: " 'Don't ask me,' Ronald shouted, 'how I feel about things as a Catholic. To me, being Catholic is part of my human existence. I don't feel one way as a human being and another *as a Catholic*' " (p. 83). Matthew functions (like Seton, but to a lesser degree) as a foil to Ronald. In a scene juxtaposed with the Marlene encounter discussed above, we see Matthew prepare for Elsie's arrival with the most improbable sophistries, which stem from the discontinuity of belief and practice in his life. In contrast to Ronald's brave struggles for integration, Matthew seldom exercises his will, relying instead on the prophylactic of onion breath. With a shrewd (but affectionate) convert's eye, Spark records all his mental shambling and scuffling. Popular Catholicism has a tendency to read the direct and therefore miraculous intervention of God in circumstances that, with Occam's razor to hand, can be accounted for adequately in other terms: "Was there not another onion left in the box? Matthew decided that this would be the testing point: if there was a miraculous onion in the vegetable box which could be used in the supper he would, before he went to fetch Elsie from the bus, eat the raw onion he had peeled upon the table . . ." (p. 52). The mock-heroic of this little episode, with its stress on enfeebled vegetables, both literal and human, mocks Matthew's habit of transference, especially since God has a divine joke up His sleeve. Elsie, otherwise unattracted, is seduced by his onion breath because it recalls an earlier lover. Tempting God (the onion has been made into a testing point), Matthew is himself led into temptation. A faith that separates dogma and action, and that turns a weazen onion into a portent from the other world, is a faith as irresponsible to the demands of matter as spiritualism itself.

Now that the major characters have been established (none the less vividly for the minimal means she has employed), Spark turns to her central plot, the trial of Patrick Seton. Chapter 4 begins inside his mind, an unusual place for the narrator to be. As Whittaker has

7. "The Deceptions of Muriel Spark," 102.

remarked apropos of the satiric pastiche in *Territorial Rights,* "an interior point of view" is a feature Spark "normally omits."[8] The reason is not hard to find. Favoring a dispassionate epigrammatic method, she tends to recoil from the "mess" of unmediated consciousness and prefers wrapping up her characters' thoughts for them, or presenting them in crisp stichomythic dialogue. Even here, where she is attempting to create an interior monologue, the result lacks the cursiveness usually found in the mode. Indeed, although the mind thus exposed for our scrutiny is thoroughly undistinguished, and not the sort that usually deals in aphorisms, the monologue becomes almost "epigrammatic" by virtue of its shorthand. Ellipses, subheadings, and disconnected paragraphs combine to give it its odd flavor. Spark allows Seton no real thoughtfulness and describes him as feeling rather than reasoning through his position:

> Patrick sat in his room . . . and thought. Or rather, he sat, and felt his thoughts.
> It was the unfortunate occurrence.
> Freda Flower: danger. (p. 57)

Perhaps the stop and start of the monologue is also meant to suggest that the speaker is infantile, incapable of any sustained flow of thought. Such infantility is confirmed by Seton's relationship with Fergusson, the policeman who functions as a father figure and also provides contact with the reality that Seton's spiritualism de facto undervalues. Fergusson, like Mortimer in *Memento Mori,* is a secular touchstone. Accustomed to the vaporousness of his own religion, Seton feels reassured by what he terms the policeman's worldliness, although it is not worldliness in the materialistic sense, but common sense that Fergusson embodies. He deals with the facts of Seton's fraudulence, not the emptiness of the fraud, with evidence that will stand in a court of law, not with tapelike ectoplasm or ectoplasmic tape.

Ideally, matter and spirit should be fused, as Ronald manages to fuse them. We have already noted how opposed he is to Manichaean dissociations of one from the other, and how he persistently attempts to bridge them. More than one commentator has allegorized his surname—Bridges—and drawn out its pontifical implications. This is why he resents his friends for investing him with oracular powers, assuming as they do that his epilepsy affects his claim to an ordinary humanity. The scene that ends the chapter shows how he

8. *Faith and Fiction,* 149.

rejects the vatic role they have thrust upon him. He is, after all, a graphologist, a professional astute enough and knowledgeable enough to take the witness stand in the trial of Seton. He knows about inks and paper and creases and any number of additional hard facts that his job requires him to assess and make inferences from. His epilepsy is not the spiritual privilege that his friends superstitiously think it is—"Ronald felt he was regarded by his friends as a sacred cow or wise monkey" (p. 67). It is true that his seizures analogically balance the medium's convulsions in the design of the novel, but, as Judy Little has observed, his "similarity to Seton is there mainly to draw attention to all the contrasts between the two."[9] As if to parallel the meeting of Seton and Fergusson (the spiritualist consulting the world), Spark ends the chapter with a scene in which Martin Bowles drives Ronald through London and asks him to apply his seer's gift to unravelling the mind of Seton (the world consulting the spiritualist). If anyone *were* capable of penetrating the mind of a fraud, it is Martin Bowles, whose behavior toward Isobel exactly counterpoints Seton's toward Alice. He is too obtuse to be aware of the ironic parallel, however, and needs Ronald to give him "mystic" information about his moral double. Such deference, as the dehumanizing animal similes show, proves an irritation to a man whose life-effort has, in vocational terms, been directed at normalizing and integrating a disability—at being a "first-rate epileptic." Like Fanny Price in *Mansfield Park,* Ronald is consulted and confided in at great cost to himself. His desire for unobtrusiveness is constantly thwarted by the conspicuity and difference that his friends confer upon him. Irony is his answer to the frustration in this instance, as he offers his own epileptic symptoms to mock the cryptic and impersonal remarks that oracles usually make. Since Martin cannot make head nor tail of what Ronald is saying (trying to construe it while pretending to concentrate on traffic), Spark's irony is compounded. The delphic answer has simply added weight to Ronald's status as the mystic "other." One imagines that the barrister would have chanted his odd congratulations about the "insight" (described as a piece, as though it were some snipped-off ectoplasmic tape) even if Ronald had said something mystifying about ganders and milestones, like Mr F.'s aunt in *Little Dorrit.*

Chapter 5 of the novel is a genre interlude, expanding the account of the public house that has earlier received "Absurdist" treatment. The focus falls once more on Matthew's intemperate pursuit of

9. *Comedy and the Woman Writer: Woolf, Spark, and Feminism,* 127.

pleasure, though it is Walter Prett who now takes over from Ronald as confessor. Again we see how Matthew has severed moral conviction from practice, and we perceive also the murky reasoning with which he tries to cover up and rationalize the divorce he has made. Ronald's austere alternative of celibacy never occurs to him, and it certainly is not suggested by his nonce-confessor. The difference between the two men is very great indeed. Whereas Ronald tries scrupulously to live by the demands of his faith (however exorbitant they might seem), Walter, also a Catholic, prides himself on an "aristocratic" moral freedom, contrasted with bourgeois enslavement to norms. Although she is clearly amused by this arrogance, Spark has little patience with antinomianism (as Bernard Harrison has observed).[10] By accusing him of cowardice, Walter is in fact accusing Matthew of failure to sin with Faustian conviction rather than of sinning at all. He does not confront Matthew's failure to wrestle with the issue at its source—his will. And his behavior in the rest of the scene, as when he utters insults based on notions of "commonness," shows him at his Waugh-like worst. His rudeness compares unfavorably with Ronald's tactful way of responding to people worlds apart from himself—whether it be Marlene with all her antagonism or Matthew in all the abjectness of his muddle. The "mock-confession" (with Walter in the booth) functions as an antimasque to a later colloquy with Ronald as confessor.

At this point of the novel, Matthew's attraction to Alice Dawes has become a monomania, a fact evident in the almost Homeric obsessiveness with which he describes her long black hair. And again, as with Martin, Ronald occupies a marginal position vis-à-vis his friend's self-absorption:

> "It's the duty of all of us to marry," Matthew said. "Isn't it? There are two callings, Holy Orders and Holy Matrimony, and one must choose."
>
> "Must one?" Ronald said. "It seems evident to me that there's no compulsion to make a choice. You are talking about life. It isn't a play."
>
> "I'm only repeating the teaching of the Church," Matthew said.
>
> "It isn't official doctrine," Ronald said. "There's no moral law against being simply a bachelor. Don't be so excessive."
>
> "One can't go on sleeping with girls and going to confession."
>
> "That's a different question," Ronald said. "That's sex: we were talking of marriage. You want your sex and don't want to marry. You never get all you want in life." (p. 80)

10. "Muriel Spark and Jane Austen," 229.

The difference between the two men becomes apparent in their respective attitudes toward the authority of the Church and the proper direction of the sexual impulse. Matthew is uncritically conformist—he recalls tags from confirmation class without a proper sense of their context or implication, whereas Ronald substitutes claims of realism for his friend's stylized, absolute pronouncements. The finality of Matthew's "It's the duty of us all to marry" is met with a Socratic question and a clear-sighted alternative; the idea of there being only two callings clearly has no place in a novel concerned with extending and humanizing the concept of vocation. Ronald's efforts to be a first-rate epileptic show that callings are in fact as various as life itself, and it is precisely because Matthew's doctrine *fails* to connect with his own life that it has all the didactic absoluteness of a morality play. In a manner befitting his function as confessor and consultant, Ronald is called upon to clarify the muddle in which Matthew's oversimplified, segregated theology on the one hand, and his casuistic abuse of the confessional on the other, have landed him. The claims of body and spirit have been dichotomized in a way essentially foreign to Spark's idea of Christian doctrine. Her article "The Religion of an Agnostic" complains about the way in which some contemporary Christian novelists have had the spirit triumph over the flesh "by virtue of disembodiment": "an amoral conception of the spirit."[11] Ronald, by contrast, though his analytic clarity might be seen on one level to dissect rather than to fuse, stands for the proper resolution of these faculties, their interinanimation, to borrow a word from Donne. We have seen this already in Ronald's impassioned response when asked to give an opinion *as a Catholic*. His Catholicism is so fully absorbed that it colors his vision and makes any sort of provisional detachment impossible. Matthew's thought, on the other hand, being externally derived rather than worked through, cannot connect with his feelings, and the severance issues in a "dissociated" sensibility. He lacks Ronald's ability to canalize feeling through creed in such a way that it embraces the whole of his being. It is thus possible to challenge Phyllis Grosskurth's view of the novels when she claims that for their author, "the supernatural is the only validity, and if people act as though chairs and human relationships have concrete reality, they are living on illusions."[12] This, it goes without

11. "The Religion of an Agnostic: A Sacramental View of the World in the Writings of Marcel Proust," 1.
12. "The World of Muriel Spark," 63.

saying, substitutes either/or for the emphatic both/and that is implicit in Ronald's declaration. As Spark herself puts it in another context, "a sacramental view of life ... is nothing more than a balanced regard for matter and spirit."[13]

The poise and depth of Ronald's perceptions are realized not only in formal debates with Matthew such as the one above, but also in his various observations made from the margins of life to which his friends (and, be it said, his condition) have relegated him. Spark endorses them by making them seem continuous with her own. When, for example, we first encounter Alice, the author draws attention to the histrionic quality of her gestures, a clutching of the throat and other items of body language that have been learned at drama school and appliquéd onto situations of stress. This self-conscious heightening is in its small way comparable to the drugs that Seton takes to enhance his trances, and it calls the sincerity of her feelings into question, as Ronald himself perceives when he meets her:

> "I shall never believe he's guilty," she said. "Never."
> Ronald thought, "How that second, histrionic 'never' diminishes her—how it debases this striking girl to a commonplace."
> "I'll always believe in his innocence," she said. "Always. No matter what the evidence is." (p. 85)

Just as he has rebuked Matthew for reducing life (with its multiplicity of options) to a theatrical "choice of Hercules," so here Ronald detects in Alice's novelettish dialogue a fission between feeling and feeler. Her self-consciousness leads her to see and applaud herself as a participant in a "drama." Because Ronald's insight duplicates earlier omniscient commentary from the author, he acquires a special authoritativeness. Indeed, it is possible to infer that the clairvoyance which people like Martin Bowles have attributed to him is the fruit of observation made accurately from the sidelines of life.

In Alice's unreflecting, self-induced conviction of Seton's innocence we also see an example of false faith, faith that fails to integrate the intellect with the feelings but instead regards them as contrarieties. Its faulty basis is to some extent measured by the feebleness and secularity of its object—Seton in all his squalor—and by her credal language later in the exchange: "I believe it, and I do believe it and I always will, always." This is not far removed from

13. "The Religion of an Agnostic," 1.

the Catholic affirmation *Et nunc, et semper* that confirms every utterance of the *Gloria Patri*.

As Alice comes to obsess Matthew, so more and more does his anxiety about his lifestyle and the opposing obligation of marriage. The debate with Ronald is resumed, and once again Spark sets quiet, ineluctable logic against intemperateness:

> "I think the spiritualists have sex. . . . I'm afraid we are heretics," he said, "or possessed by devils. . . . It shows a dualistic attitude, not to marry if you aren't going to be a priest or a religious. You've got to affirm the oneness of reality in some form or another."
>
> "We're not in fact heretics," Ronald said, "under the correct meaning of the term."
>
> "Well, we've got an heretical attitude, in a way."
>
> "Not in fact. But does it worry you?"
>
> "Yes."
>
> "Do you want to marry?"
>
> "No."
>
> "Then you've got a problem . . . ." (pp. 89–90)

One of the ironies here is the way in which, to draw comfort from numbers, Matthew includes Ronald in his dilemma through the first person plural and implicitly accuses his friend of having the "dualistic" attitude that Ronald's catechizing has laid bare in himself. The antithesis is not the antithesis of holy orders and marriage that Matthew sets up as an Aunt Sally of comforting impossibility, but of celibacy and marriage—that is, of surrendering to, or sanctifying, the sexual urge.

The clarity of Ronald's perceptions in this and other issues carries in it the seeds of pride, and the author later forces him to regard in another sufferer the condition it has been his life's vocation to face and endure. While he has resolved Matthew's crisis to its essence, his mastery of his own condition is not entire. Earlier in the novel he has smiled at himself in a plate-glass window when Matthew congratulates him on his memory (memory is Ronald's talisman against the mental decay associated with his disease); now we see him recoil inhumanly from a fellow epileptic. Self-applause has yielded to a stricken sense of impotence. *The Cloud of Unknowing* is a treatise on spirituality important enough for Spark to quote in *The Hothouse by the East River*, and it has this to say about the pride which Ronald's encounter with the epileptic serves to arraign: "You are to consider yourself even more wretched and accursed, unless by grace and by direction you do all that in you lies, to live according to your calling."[14] The epileptic as he lies on the pavement becomes not so much a *memento mori* as a *memento pati*: "'I doubt if I can do it,' Ronald said. He was greatly agitated, for if there was one thing he did not like to see it was another epileptic. The thought of touching the man horrified him. . . . Ronald felt for the shoes as one thrusting his hands into flames. He shut his eyes, and felt for the laces . . ." (p. 91).

That the experience is purgatorial can be gathered from the imagery of flames—possibly suggested by the fact that Cranmer thrust his hand into fire to expiate his recantation. Instead of a self-congratulatory reflection, Ronald is seeing his frailty mirrored in the impotent man, not so much *capax rationis* as animallike, drumming his feet like a horse. The confrontation shakes him, but, true to his usual practice of remaining conscious during fits, he does not take drugs to ward off the seizure it is likely to induce. His reward is a "living troubled sleep instead of a dead and peaceful one," epithets which suggest that life and trouble are nearly synonymous. Indeed, a Catholic hymn to the Virgin, the Salve Regina, goes so far as to describe the sublunary world as a *vallis lacrimarum*. The presence of such dark assumptions in the fiction has led some critics to brand it "anti-humanist," though of course any examination of *The Bachelors* will show the charge to be wide of the mark, however much it might apply to some of the later novels.

Ronald is chastened by reminders of the divine will that inscrutably extends beyond his own; Patrick Seton uses blackmail to impose his will upon others. Juxtaposed with Ronald's humiliating encounter is a scene in which Seton blackmails Dr. Lyte, guilty of a woman's death through abortion. It is implied that evil alone confers power on the blackmailer, for when Seton visits Inspector Fergusson, the disparity between the two men, one with integrity, one without, becomes clear. The doctor's abjectness in the face of evil manipulation is at once displaced by evil's own abjectness in the face of unmanipulable (because invulnerable) good. Seton cowers before the inspector, his gauche discomfiture like a schoolboy's. Cutting back to Dr. Lyte, the narrator then tracks the impenitence of the man whom Seton has been blackmailing. His perfunctory atonement for the death of his patient ("He became a communist for a space, by way of atonement" [p. 103]) points to the materialism of

---

14. Anon., *The Cloud of Unknowing*, 118. Henceforth cited parenthetically in the text by title and page number.

his outlook, something which reveals itself also in the way he demythologizes Seton, finding criminality a more manageable alternative than demonism. In Spark's view the "empirical" hypothesis is as much an act of faith in the face of contradictory evidence, and the motives informing the choice of theory are far from noble ones; but these are things Lyte chooses not to address: "In the end, Cyril Lyte found it less frightening to believe that Patrick was a common blackmailer, and no medium between this world and the other." This authorial statement, by virtue of a definite article before the word *other,* gives an incontestible reality to the "other world." Any resolution based on the abolition of the spirit is, for Spark, as unstable as one based, like Seton's, on the abolition of matter.

When it becomes clear that, owing to Matthew's indiscretion, evidence to be used against Seton at his trial has been stolen, Ronald has a vision of human futility and worthlessness, one of several that beset him in the novel, and which give his patience and kindliness of temper an almost heroic dimension. The virtues he practices, it seems, are not spontaneous upwellings of beneficence. They have rather to be affirmed with "saddened intensity"[15] in the face of disillusionment:

> Ronald was filled with a great melancholy boredom from which he suffered periodically. It was not merely this affair which seemed to suffocate him, but the whole of life—people, small-time criminals, outraged housekeepers, and all his acquaintance from the beginning of time. When this overtook him Ronald was apt to refuse himself comfortable thoughts: on the contrary he used to tell himself: this sensation, this boredom and disgust, may later seem, in retrospect, to have been one of the happier moods of my life, so appalling may be the experiences to come. It is better, he thought, to be a pessimist in life, it makes life endurable. The slightest optimism invites disappointment. (p. 107)

This is a condition of existentialist despair, and therefore comes close to courting mortal sin. In negative "epiphanies" such as the one above, Ronald is deliberately refusing himself "comfortable thoughts." This may look like an ascetic renunciation of solace, but it also, through a resonance with the "comfortable words" in the *Book of Common Prayer,* amounts to a refusal of grace. In an effort to skirt the ungrounded optimism of Pelagius, Ronald seems to move now and again toward its dark Augustinian antitype.

Another attack of *nausée* occurs after a more than usually futile

15. Harold Schneider, "A Writer in Her Prime: The Fiction of Muriel Spark," 41.

party. On this occasion, however, Ronald does allow himself some Pauline "comfortable words" as antidote:

> His melancholy and boredom returned with such force when he was alone again in his flat that he recited to himself as an exercise against it, a passage from the Epistle to the Philippians, which was at present meaningless to his numb mind, in the sense that a coat of paint is meaningless to a window-frame, and yet both colours and preserves it: "All that rings true, all that commands reverence, and all that makes for right; all that is pure, all that is lovely, all that is gracious in the telling; virtue and merit, wherever virtue and merit are found—let this be the argument of your thoughts."
>
> For Ronald was suddenly obsessed by the party, and by the figures who had moved under Isobel's chandelier, and who, in Ronald's present mind, seemed to gesticulate like automatic animals; they had made sociable noises which struck him as hysterical. Isobel's party stormed upon him like a play in which the actors had begun to jump off the stage, so that he was no longer the witness of a comfortable satire, but was suddenly surrounded by a company of ridiculous demons.
>
> This passage from Philippians was a mental, not a spiritual exercise; a mere charm to ward off the disgust, the despair, the brain-burning.
>
> This was the beginning of November. It is the month, Ronald told himself in passing, when the dead rise up and come piling upon you to warm themselves. One is affected as if by a depressive drug, one shivers. It is only the time of year, that's the trouble. (pp. 116–17)

Ronald's spiritual crisis here is a crisis of faith not in the divine but in the human, and it issues in a sort of narcotic indifference that is unable, through disgust, to stretch forth in empathy. The ordinary human impulse would be to surrender to the state and wait for it to pass. Ronald's solution is, by an effort of will, to offset the nausea with affirmations. These are as absolute in their formulation as his disgust is absolute in its range. Ann Dobie states that in Muriel Spark's novels "refusing to define one's reality leads to emptiness and sterility,"[16] but for Ronald reality is often precisely that—empty and sterile. St. Paul's ideals are not felt by the mind in its wooden numbness, but the Herbertian simile of a window frame suggests their efficacy none the less, for the frame is the support of a view out of the claustrophobic self into the infinite divine ("A man that looks on glasse / On it may stay his eye; / Or if he pleaseth, through it passe, / And then the heav'n espie").

16. "Muriel Spark's Definition of Reality," 23.

"Demons" have first to be exorcised, though. The Absurdism already glimpsed in the obsessiveness and discontinuity of the exchanges in the public house, and embodied in the members of Ronald's circle, all entrapped within their own preoccupations, here has the force of an epiphany. They lose dimension, flattened and darkened to silhouettes by want of enlightenment. Spark denies their rationality by the phrase "automatic animals," which supplants reason with an instinctuality both beastlike and mechanical, and language, a means to human community, is suddenly recognized for the hysterical noise it has always threatened to become in such scenes as Walter Prett's reading of the diet list. The theatricality that annoys Ronald in Matthew and Alice here infects the very texture of human intercourse. What is more disquieting, however, is that once the *frame* of art has been revoked, Ronald has to endure all the artifice of theater without the reassuring control of its form, pity and terror without catharsis. The spirits of All Souls recollect the spirits of Seton's seances, and their parasitic warming of themselves on the living recalls Coleridge's "LIFE-IN-DEATH / Who thicks man's blood with cold." Here, even within the context of his faith, Ronald finds despair.

In the reference "comfortable satire" we glimpse again that detachment trenching on pride that Ronald's encounter with the epileptic called to order, and yet, when his friends force themselves upon him in all their unpleasantness, he cannot shrug them off, but rather subjects them to a formal arraignment. This summoning up of specters ("he began to abstract his acquaintance, in his mind's eye") is an ad hoc seance that parodies the seances of Patrick Seton. Evils are announced and then exorcised so that charity can reign (however feebly) over rejection. Here is one example: "Isobel Billows, with her hungry lusts, her generosity wherever she thought generosity a good investment, smiled up at him in the glaring eye of his mind" (p. 117). But, when the fit of nausea has passed, he is able to make some sort of minimal affirmation—"Isobel is brave simply to go on breathing; another woman might have committed suicide ten years ago" (p. 121). A fit succeeds these thoughts of nullity and disgust, only partly checked by the recitation of St. Paul and by the feeble instances of good he is able to invoke as counterpoise, and the sequence ends, dryly acknowledging the presence of divinity behind the spiritual torments of the *Totentanz*:

> He resolved to go to Confession, less to rid himself of the past night's
> thoughts—since his priest made a distinction between sins of thought

and these convulsive dances and dialogues of the mind—than to receive absolution, a friendly gesture of recognition from the maker of heaven and earth, vigilant manipulator of the Falling Sickness. (pp. 121–22)

Since Ronald has not willed his uncharitable thoughts—they have, on the contrary, stormed upon him—his visit to the Confessional is not to purge a sin, but to find assurance in the attentiveness of God. He is consoled by the fact that, through the Incarnation, even so distant and inscrutable a Deity as the "maker of heaven and earth" is able to "recognize" him in his human frailty and is able to shape, to "manipulate," pattern out of the contingent evil of sickness, whose Falling is not simply the lapse of the Fall, but also the inability of human beings to do the impossible—to reach heaven by an effort of unaided will. In the words of *The Cloud of Unknowing*, "after each impulse, because of the corruption of the flesh, the soul falls down again to some thought or some deed done or undone" (p. 126). Ronald's epilepsy leaves the realm of the contingent and enters the realm of symbol by virtue of the wider applicability the uppercase letters have given it.

The remaining part of the novel sustains its structure of symmetries and equivalences. Trying to imitate Alice, Elsie has found *her* Seton in a spiritualist "priest," whose ordination is based on an improperly self-made form of faith—"He was a real priest, he told her, ordained by no man-made bishop but by Fire and the Holy Ghost" (p. 128). This claim, denying the *omnes generationes* implicit in the apostolic succession, is a sterile one, its sterile nature further mirrored by his homosexuality. Since Elsie realizes that he has been exploiting her and exposes him, the symmetry is to some extent inverted, for Alice will never discover the comparable fraudulence of Seton. But the parallelism is reinstated in the paternal attitude Father Socket adopts toward his protegé Mike Garland, this resembling (and counterpointing) the filiation of Seton and Inspector Fergusson.

Chapter 10, near the meridian of the novel, reverts to the panoramic mode of the opening and close, cutting from generality to particular, or, as Peter Kemp has put it, to "damningly epitomizing scenes."[17] In this case the epitome contains much of the affair between Tim and Hildegarde. Her self-regarding fuss over Ronald is seen to persist even after he has left her, a fuss the anaphoric repetitions serve to underline:

17. *Muriel Spark*, 62.

"I used to mend all Ronald's clothes. I used to buy the theatre tickets. I used to rush to his flat after my work and—"

"I know," said Tim, "you told me." And he plugged in his electric razor, the noise of which drowned her voice. (p. 143)

Ronald, in a scene juxtaposed with this, is seen coming out of church. Affronted by the priest's paternal manner (the shadow of Hildegarde's maternity), he calls his condescension into question:

"Well, Tom," said the priest. "Well, Mary, and how's your mother?"

"A bit better, thank you, Father."

"Well, Ronald," said this very young priest as Ronald came out.

"Well, Sonny," Ronald said.

The young priest stared after Ronald as he rapidly walked his way, then remembered Ronald Bridges was an epileptic, and turned to the next comer. (p. 144)

The priest here proves as obtuse as Martin in connecting Ronald's rudeness with his epilepsy, and almost deserves the sharp retort he has received. Spark has invested the scene with great comic value, a value partly based on its unexpectedness, for it presents Ronald in an uncharacteristically harsh mood. It is the first instance of an authorial frustration with priests that will reach a climax in *The Takeover*. Considered apart from his office, this man is simply the utterer of bland, meaningless chitchat. And his response to Ronald's disorder provides yet another instance of the epileptic's isolation from society—his treatment as an oddity by friend and stranger alike.

This isolation naturally enough equips Ronald for the confessional, and the role of confessor is one that we have seen him occupy with authenticity and compassion. Flanking accounts of Martin's relations with Isobel and Ewart's with Marlene throw his kindness into relief. The detachment with which they view each woman in turn points to coldness and self-sufficiency. Both are incapable of reciprocal feeling, for they regard their partners as encumbrances to be exploited and then sacrificed to convenience. Indeed, their selfishness in the face of suffering is tinged with sadism: "She was crying, and it satisfied him to see her cry, and to have brought about this drooping of her stately neck . . ." (p. 156).

Such scenes prepare the way for Ronald's moving encounter with Elsie, where his integrity and selflessness come to the fore. Also crucial to this dialogue, which turns upon his clear-sightedness, is a passage delineating the mental habits of Seton. We have often seen Ronald hone his memory, not only to keep epileptic "deterioration" at bay, but also because it is with facts, unsentimentally perceived, that he is accustomed to deal. Seton, by contrast, is an "impressionist," blurring facts into an all-absorbing subjectivity. He also resembles Ewart and Martin in his impassive response to suffering:

> Patrick sat in his calm, watching her, and he experienced that murmuring in his mind which was his memory. He could not recall where he had seen a similar sight before, but he felt he had. His memory was impressionistic, formed of a few indistinguishable sensations among a mass of cloudy matter generally forming his past. . . . "All round your hand you are aware of objects—you see them, but not distinctly. What you see round the palm of your hand is an *impression*." Patrick's memory had become this type of impression . . . . (pp. 170–71)

The imagery supporting this analysis is drawn in part from spiritualism, the "mass of cloudy matter" again suggesting ectoplasm. At the same time the teacher's explanation of impressionist art becomes a parable of solipsism, the palm acting as a blinker against engagement with the outer world, which drizzles in round the edges of a huge self-absorption. Matter—the matter which Spark sees encompassed in a combination of "heavenly ideas with earthly things"[18] —is also sacrificed in Seton's exalting "poetry" (viz., Yeats) above law: "I think, said Patrick, people should read more poetry and dream their dreams, and I do not recognize man-made laws and dogmas" (p. 172). This echoes Father Socket's contempt for "man"-made bishops and Marlene's arbitrary proceedings within her spiritualist circle, and it stands in opposition to Ronald's respect for the reality that is the vector of the divine. Although she is not a circumstantial novelist, Spark sets her early works in clearly realized settings and spaces. And even when she experiments with faceless urban settings and purgatorial nonentities in the middle period, her techniques cannot be termed "impressionistic." "Minimalist" would better describe the effort of compression, the striving for *multum in parvo*.

I have already noted that Ronald's encounter with Elsie is central to the novel—not so much from the point of view of its plot, since Ronald's evidence, based on the letter he has managed to retrieve, does not carry much weight in convicting Seton—but because it shows disinterested generosity on the part of both protagonists, a generosity far beyond the self-enclosedness of Martin Bowles, Ewart

18. Spark, "The Mystery of Job's Suffering: Jung's New Interpretation Examined," 7.

Thornton, or even Matthew Finch. Ronald's flexibility is illustrated by his being touched rather than repelled by the mannerisms Elsie has picked up from Alice, for he perceives the pathos of the imitation:

> "I've faced it already," she said with tragic intensity, such as Alice employed when talking to a man, and the stress of the occasion demanded it.
> All at once, Ronald quite liked her.
> "I have died," she said, "many deaths."
> "Tell me," he said, "how that has happened." (p. 177)

The theatrical exaggeration of Elsie's metaphor is, in a kindly way, pointed by Ronald's question, which marks the start of the education she receives in the course of their dialogue—a maieutic education like the one that Matthew has received at his hands. With Ronald the usual pattern of Elsie's relationships is altered, and he offers her the mutuality of discourse instead of sexual exploitation. The relief she feels becomes apparent in the readiness and in the detailed nature of her confidences:

> "I have had sex without any relationships. I don't know why I'm telling you this the first five minutes."
> "You've met the wrong chaps," Ronald said.
> "All the chaps are the wrong ones. If they aren't married they are queer; if they aren't queer, they are hard; if they aren't hard they are soft. I can't get anywhere with men, somehow. Why am I telling you all this?"
> "I'm the uncle type," Ronald said. (p. 177)

The homosexual Father Socket has exploited Elsie no less than the men who have unfeelingly bedded her; Ronald provides a contrast with both kinds in his disinterestedness. He emerges as the Aristotelian mean between the categories of hardness (loveless sexuality) and softness (manipulative, Setonian gentleness) into which Elsie has slotted her male acquaintance. His balance inspires the confidence his marginal position in life—a consequence of his epileptic "vocation"—has always ensured. The joke about being an "uncle" has as much pathos as it has wit, endorsed as it is by his cues and advice in the conversation that follows. Thus when Elsie tries to align him with her previous exploiters, she fails. Instead of using her, Ronald tells her about the nature of agapaic love:

> "Well, you've got a nerve, I'll say that. But you all come for what you can get."

"Give it to me for love," Ronald said. "The best type of love to give is sacrificial. It's an embarrassing type of love to receive, if that's any consolation to you. The best type of love that you can receive is to be taken for granted as a dependable person and otherwise ignored— that's more comfortable." (p. 183)

We are reminded in this apparently prosaic testimony of St. Paul's great hymn to Charity in 2 Corinthians 13 and even of Christ's definition of love as the sacrifice of life. Ronald leaves with the letter that Elsie has stolen from him and, in refusing to sleep with her, helps by practical example to focus the meaning of their exchange. Its effect is profound, and in a comically tabular way, she later applies his analytic method to the untidiness of her life:

"No, it's Crown property, excuse me. But it's his forgery, all right. Five, if you don't believe Patrick forged the letter I don't see what you're worried about. . . ."
"Oh, shut up," said Alice, "with your one, two, three, four, five. You're such a clever cookie since you saw that man . . . ." (pp. 187–88)

Of course Elsie, having been introduced to notions of integrity and disinterestedness, does not all at once turn into a saint, as her trying to manipulate Ronald on p. 207 reveals. But, that relapse notwithstanding, she *does* testify at the trial of Seton and, discrediting one of his character witnesses, is instrumental in securing his conviction.

Ronald has thus helped a woman whose life on her own admission has been meaningless to find an intrinsic purpose. His tactful role as catalyst to self-realization contrasts with the blatant way in which Hildegarde, his former lover, attempted to take over his life and reduce him to infantile dependence. This is why Spark inserts the detail of Hildegarde's reconversion to Catholicism after the interview with Elsie. We are meant to see her spiritual life as the mere adjunct of the relationships to which it is subordinated. Ronald, in a truly Pauline way, has tried to be all things to all people, his flexibility centered by his commitment to his faith. Hildegarde, on the other hand, has been all people to all things, her echo-chamber hollowness displayed by her doing the right thing for the wrong reason (T. S. Eliot's words):

"What a good memory you've got. Did she join under your influence?"
"Yes. I rather regretted it later."
"Why?"
"Because she lapsed."

"Well, she's gone back. There's definitely something odd about Hildegarde. She was a spiritualist for a time, not long ago."
"Under your influence?" (p. 190)

Influence which fails to permeate the psyche and catalyze new perceptions and nuances of consciousness is the merely manipulative influence of a Patrick Seton. It is the "deific" imposition of the will to demonstrate mere power that Ronald abhors. Ewart's behavior toward Freda over the telephone also provides an instance of influence exerted to this unsavory end. As soon as friendship requires his engagement, he withdraws. His relationships, empty colloquies over telephones, are mediumistic too in their fatal deficiency of matter: " 'I should like to see you. Won't you come over?' 'Sorry. Loads of homework' " (p. 198).

When the book climaxes in the trial scene, and Ronald has an epileptic fit after taking the witness stand, the parallel with his demonic antitype is finally made clear. Seton, who in a seance has placed himself low on the chain of being by his cry "I creep" (p. 202), ironically sustains himself throughout the cross-examination with thoughts of omnipotence—"I will look down on her, he thought, when she is lying on the mountainside, and the twitching will cease" (p. 222)—an example of what J. Dierickx has called the "Promethean" sin of "emulating the Maker in a creation of his own."[19] Ronald, on the other hand, is presented almost allegorically as an exemplum of fallible humanity, something shown by his scrupulous, literal response to the cross-questioning: " 'Mr. Bridges, have you ever made a mistake?' 'Yes,' said Ronald" (p. 221). His epileptic fit in the midst of his evidence has much the same function. It acknowledges human limitation, where Seton's trances and *vaticinia* claim superhuman transcendence. And bringing in its wake a recurrence of the melancholy and boredom we have earlier seen Ronald trying to ward off with a text, it puts the sordid, manipulative reality of the trial *sub specie jusititiae divinae*. The asyndetic list of the three men at the start of the extract allows them to fuse with each other, the implication being that they are all aspects of the same evil:

Martin Bowles, Patrick Seton, Socket.
And the others as well, rousing him up: fruitless souls, crumbling tinder, like his own self which did not bear thinking of. But it is all demonology, he thought, and he brought them all to witness, in his old style, one by one before the courts of his mind. (p. 240)

19. J. Dierickx, "A Devil Figure in a Contemporary Setting: Some Aspects of Muriel Spark's 'The Ballad of Peckham Rye,'" 21.

It is a bleak conclusion for the novel, perhaps, but it is also a chastened one. If in an access of Jansenist gloom Ronald can see his friends only in terms of the sterility of bachelorhood, he is humble enough to include himself in the indictment. And we have enough conviction of his strength and goodness of character to feel sure that the mood will pass and that the words from Philippians will come finally to exert their power. For if *The Bachelors* affirms anything at all, it affirms that Ronald has achieved a sort of holiness through submitting the self to the divine, not as a priest but as a person. His vocation, in which his very selfhood inheres, finally ensures that he will ring true, command reverence, and make for right.

2

The Girls of Slender Means
Divine Vocation

The vocation of Nicholas Farringdon in *The Girls of Slender Means* is a conventionally religious one (unlike Ronald's in *The Bachelors*), though the novel treats the topic in a roundabout way, and the event that secures his submission to God is preceded by an account of the hostel in which it occurs and of the girls who live there. Yet, while the book might seem to resolve into episodes of tender reminiscence, of nostalgia for an irrecoverable phase of innocence, the author ensures that even its most random details are subsumed to its theological center and that we never lose sight of the human deficiencies which are made into channels of grace. This thematic economy, and the tendentiousness of its most innocent-seeming detail, become apparent at the very start:

> Long ago in 1945 all the nice people in England were poor, allowing for exceptions. The streets of the city were lined with buildings in bad disrepair or in no repair at all, bomb-sites piled with stony rubble, houses like giant teeth in which decay had been drilled out, leaving only the cavity. Some bomb-ripped buildings looked like the ruins of ancient castles until, at a closer view, the wallpapers of various quite normal rooms would be visible, room above room, exposed, as on a stage, with one wall missing; sometimes a lavatory chain would dangle over nothing from a fourth- or fifth-floor ceiling; most of all the staircases survived, like a new art-form, leading up and up to an unspecified destination that made unusual demands on the mind's eye.[1]

Spark begins by associating a romance formula ("Long ago") with the specificity of "1945," a year that saw the end of history's most terrible episode, and it is from this tension (subsisting between the

---

1. Spark, *The Girls of Slender Means*, 1. Hereafter cited parenthetically in the text by page number.

ideal and the reality it sacrifices to itself) that the book comes into being. Nicholas's conversion is, after all, partly caused by the discrepancy between Romantic perceptions and the savage actuality they blur, a discrepancy evident from the start. The year 1945 is close enough to our times for the "Long ago" to function thematically rather than literally, resonating as it does, say, with the "ages long ago" in *The Eve of St Agnes*. Spark uses the formula (hinting the unreality of romance) to prepare us for the aphorism that follows, not the less wittily exorbitant for its rider—"allowing for exceptions"—for it is on the strength of such exceptions that Nicholas's judgment of the hostel goes awry.

A rhythm of glamorous claim and sober retraction recurs throughout the otherwise "atmospheric" description of the city. In this context, the noun one would ordinarily expect after the verb *lined* is *trees*, but the buildings that Spark substitutes are not only discomfittingly unpastoral, but also in a state of collapse. She suggests their vacuity by the suspended nonapplicability of the phrase "in no repair at all," which is left dangling like the lavatory chain. In the same way, the simile of the drilled teeth seems at first to promise restoration, but this is canceled by their being left unfilled. The strategy of negation also crops up in the way Spark overturns the romance of ruins, substituting the wreckage of domestic villas, with their paraphernalia of wallpapers and lavatory chains.

The reader is being prepared by this repeated stress on precariousness and vulnerability for the accident at the boarding house, not least by the references to surviving staircases, which, terminating in the sky, suggest Jacob's ladder and Nathanael's vision as much as they do the nightmarish inventions of Piranesi. They also anticipate the want of an escape route when the bomb explodes. The mind's eye, taxed in construing a destination for the climber of those staircases, will later coincide with Nicholas's eye of faith as he sees Selina emerge and Joanna fall with the ruin, as baffling a problem for faith as the diverging destinations of body and spirit. Joseph Hynes has pointed out that when "Joanna and the building go down together, after a whole bookful of her recitations of poems . . . concerned with death and resurrection, the reader harks back to those opening words contrasting decay and collapse to ascending staircases, open sky and regions of the imagination."[2] Spark's refrain about the poverty of nice people recurs at this point—many of her novels have a touch of balladry—but its epigrammatic repleteness is

2. *Art of the Real*, 60.

now qualified and opened up, the romance perception troubled by the reality it has excluded from its frame: "All the nice people were poor; at least, that was a general axiom, the best of the rich being poor in spirit" (p. 1).

The evil to which the ruin of London testifies is presented as an evil so great that it defies human conception and human response. Ordinary conversations have to skirt it for the more conceivable topics of architecture and weather. It will be Nicholas's fate likewise to witness more conceivable instances of that same evil (continuous with the Nazi atrocities and the carnage of war, but fixed within a more manageable compass).

As we move from the survey of the city to the hostel itself, Spark uses the passive voice to create a general context for her specific portraits. This has the effect of regulating the girls' lives as if by natural law, in terms of which the individual will must forge its identity. Again and again in the novel the author stresses the tension between fashion and selfhood, imposed and self-made order. It is not so much the board of the May of Teck Club that is inspecting the windows, replacing the glass, and removing the bitumous paint, but a sort of genius loci that blends into the *dea abscondita* of the author herself, as she moves from these documentary details into her epigrammatic mode and converts windows into symbols, barriers between domestic normality and the war, *signifiants* of life itself. Her reference to the "final reckoning," while it might seem to be pointing to the apocalyptic climax of the war, is just as pertinent to the fire at the hostel. And in that fire we witness an inverted type of the Last Judgment and see the physically, not the spiritually, beautiful pass through a lavatory window that parodies the needle's eye, as William McBrien has pointed out.[3] Similarly, the war "going on" outside the confines of normal domestic life, and yet obtruding on it every time its brittle defense is breached, is the eternal battle of good and evil soon to be miniaturized in the events surrounding the fire. One of the author's seamless transitions from general to illustrative particular can be seen in the way she describes the view from the windows of the hostel, where the windows themselves hinge the swing of the topic, much as the Albert Memorial has pivoted a change of material on the preceding page. Once again, what seems to be a documentary purpose is compounded with a prophetic one as we gauge the height of the building (it will prevent Joanna from jumping) by the Lowry-like perspective it offers on the

3. "Muriel Spark: The Novelist as Dandy," 167.

street. The refrain about poverty and niceness crops up yet again, and now leads us out of London into the collective mind of the hostel. General references continue to keep us at a distance, inviting us to judge the self-absorption and the hedonism of the girls whose thoughts, far from dwelling on the Four Last Things the writer has repeatedly brought to mind, are caught up in a childlike, pastoral present. Peter Pan's Kensington Gardens, after all, are not very far away:

> All the nice people were poor, and few were nicer, as nice people come, than these girls at Kensington who glanced out of the windows in the early mornings to see what the day looked like, or gazed out on the green summer evenings . . . . few people alive at the time were more delightful, more ingenious, more movingly lovely, and, as it might happen, more savage, than the girls of slender means. (pp. 3–4)

The synesthetic transference of green from foliage to light and ultimately time itself in the phrase "green evenings" shows the girls' dwelling in present experience (and in a Barrie-esque milieu) and also points to their immaturity. They are "green girls" in the obsolete meaning of that phrase, and rapt in the contemplation of their loveliness. At the same time, however, we glimpse the self-seeking that goes hand in hand with narcissism. V. M. K. Kelleher has indicated that "the 'slender means' of the title carry strong suggestions of an almost holy poverty. But their means are slender in another sense: beneath the youthful ebullience, there lurks a spiritual poverty, an unthinking animal self-centeredness. This sinister undertone is continually hinted at, and is finally revealed at the moment of crisis, in Selina's 'action of savagery.'"[4] What Nicholas encounters at the May of Teck Club will anticipate the savagery of Haiti, and both will serve as paradoxical instruments of divine grace.

It is to Nicholas's martyrdom on the Caribbean island that the narrative focus now shifts, and Spark, relying on the nonconsecutive tessellation of events that she had perfected in the preceding novel, *The Prime of Miss Jean Brodie*, cuts to a present from which the happenings of 1945 are only dimly remembered. She has observed in a recent interview: "I play around a great deal with time, for instance; in some of my books I do away with time altogether. What interests me about time is that I don't think chronology is causality."[5]

4. "The Religious Artistry of Muriel Spark," 87.
5. Frankel, "Interview," 451.

The *effect* on Nicholas of Joanna's death and Selina's heartless salvage has clearly gone unnoticed by other survivors—they have fixed him as "an anarchist and poet sort of thing" or "The one that got on the roof to sleep out with Selina" (p. 5). While his spirit has been transmuted by the fire, they themselves seem statically and unreflectingly to remain what they have always been—"She spoke, by habit since her debutante days, with the utmost enthusiasm of tone" (p. 5). Dorothy can gush like a travel agent even after learning of Nicholas's death (*martyred* has to be glossed for her), and her scatty equation of two distinct islands gives further point to that indifferent "turning away" that Auden has explored in his famous poem:

> "No, he's been martyred."
> "What-ed?"
> "Martyred in Haiti. Killed. . . ."
> "But I've just been to Tahiti, it's marvellous, everyone's marvellous." (p. 5)

These conversations are intercalated throughout the book—segments of unredeemed time against the patterned events of the hostel narrative. They function also as flashes forward (comparable to the more directly handled flashes in *The Prime of Miss Jean Brodie*) to show the undeveloping extension of each life out of the past into the present—Selina, we learn, has a tribe of secretaries who shield her from contact with the world, and Dorothy expresses her shattered emotions and her desire for a good gossip in the same breath.

Joanna is the first of the girls whose inward life is given to the reader in any great detail. She is not without the theatricality that, in *The Bachelors*, Spark satirizes in Alice and Elsie, but here it is redeemed by its innocent unconsciousness. She is presented as having a love of poetry comparable to a cat's of birds, stalking and gobbling her poems while she memorizes them. Poetry is conceived in terms of performance, not as objective statement, and while it becomes a part of her as a bird, once gobbled, might be said to become part of a cat, it has been reduced to a sort of impassioned *vocalise*. The concern with large emotion, and the passionate, unthoughtful idealism that goes with it, mark Joanna as a Romantic. Spark does not usually approve of Romantics, for, as Derek Stanford has noted, "she rejects the cult of inflated personality,"[6] but her treatment of Joanna is by no means wholly satiric. Indeed the writer blames her excessiveness on her education. Joanna exemplifies not

---

6. *Muriel Spark*, 93.

so much the inflation of personality as that Romantic oblation of the self before a cause—she quotes Byron's lines on Marathon, for example, on p. 108. Such self-immolation is dubious because, unlike Christian martyrdom, it calls attention to the self at the very moment of its denial. It has a showiness as unrealistic as the mistaking of bomb-ravaged suburbia for ancient castles, or Selina for an exemplar of holy poverty. To this degree Joanna's exaltation of art above life incurs the narrator's displeasure:

> All her ideas of honour and love came from the poets. She was vaguely acquainted with distinctions and sub-distinctions of human and Divine love, and their various attributes, but this was picked up from rectory conversations when theologically-minded clerics came to stay; it was in a different category of instruction from ordinary household beliefs such as the axiom, "People are holier who live in the country," and the notion that a nice girl should only fall in love once in her life. (pp. 21–22)

The intensity of Joanna's imaginative life (as revealed through her obsession with poetry) is accompanied by vagueness about the reality outside it, an innocent parallel to Seton's "impressionism." Such crucial distinctions as that between divine and human love have failed to impinge on her with any force during her childhood in a country parish. The oppressive and suffocating idealisms that her father has imposed on her are rendered as an atmospheric pressure of the soul. Joanna's father, visiting London after her death, goes so far as to suggest that Christianity itself has fled the cities. Having fled with it, he implicitly prides himself on a fugitive and cloistered virtue—proof that he has been responsible for thwarting his daughter's development. The effect of all this on her emotional life is unfortunate, since, after one disappointment in love, she feels compelled to renounce all relationships.

Joanna bases her decision on the absolutes of "Let me not to the marriage of true minds," confusing the permanence of sacred with the transience of profane love: "Once you admit that you can change the object of a strongly-felt affection, you undermine the whole structure of love and marriage, the whole philosophy of Shakespeare's sonnet" (p. 22). Intemperate positions omit a sense of growth, and the fixity of Joanna's beliefs, however attractively innocent, strikes a note of callowness. This can be seen also in her preference for declamatory verse, and in the way she has allowed vocal performance to displace experience. The man she sacrifices to her ideal is similarly shown to be immature through want of a tempering exposure to life: "he was yet inexperienced in many respects, although he later learned some reality as an Air Force chaplain" (p. 25). The sermon he preaches in the country parish, with its Greek exegesis, and its high-flown claims, is clearly preached more for the benefit of himself than of the rustic congregation, who, without the slightest intention of plucking them out as he urges them to, stare at him with round impassive eyes. Self-immolation is much more the province of people who sentimentalize the country than of country people themselves.

The "vocation" of Joanna is consequently the stillborn offspring of a sterile resolve; it has only a false Romanticism to invest it with meaning. Spark's stress on sensation suggests a displaced physicality, while her precision about fees (poetry Benthamitically reduced to pence) provides a touch of mock-heroic: "The sensation of poetry replaced the sensation of the curate, and she took on pupils at six shillings an hour, pending her diploma" (p. 25).

Naive though Joanna's position might be, there can be no doubting its superiority to the affected worldliness and cynicism of other boarders who devalue the emotional life. Anne Baberton speaks slightingly of her brother because that is what is expected of her, and the same false nonchalance can be detected in the manner she adopts toward her boyfriend, whom she does not greet because they have become engaged. If Joanna's "nice" upbringing has led to emotional excess, then Anne's has had a converse effect. The fault is to be found in the honor they give to false models, to fashions that are modish in the case of Anne and obsolete in the case of Joanna. Indeed fashion is felt throughout the novel as a tyrannous source of pressure, whether it dictates the possession of hair-grips or an elegant figure.

The notion of conformity also underpins sections of the book that subordinate individual characters to general overviews. One of these is the description of the VE celebrations, which is far from celebratory in tone, and which shows collective action as a menace to humanity. Spark presents it in terms of an animal stampede, an image of bestial power Lise will later see televised on many screens in *The Driver's Seat*.[7] The "press" in "self-expression" becomes literalized as the pushing out of the self into a promiscuous mass bent on its very destruction. Members of the club set out to "express themselves along with the rest of London on the victory of the war with Germany. . . . Only the St. John's Ambulance men, watchful

7. Spark, *The Driver's Seat*, 94.

beside their vans, had any identity left. . . . Many strange arms were twined round strange bodies" (pp. 14–15). That there is a sinister side to this hysteria is evident in the way in which uniform alone (in the case of the ambulance men) provides a differentia in the seething uniformity, and the manner in which the passive voice insinuates itself into the description as an emblem of mindlessness. If Joanna, by adapting her emotions to the claims of the romance tradition, is courting the death implicit in passion—Denis de Rougemont has noted that "Tristan's inclination for a *deliberate obstruction* turns out to be a desire for death and an advance in the direction of Death!"[8]—there is a different kind of death, a death of identity, implicit in the communal surge of VE Day. By describing it as a combination of a wedding and a funeral, one of the boarders articulates the ambivalence Spark feels about mass responses of this kind.

The author never lets us forget that World War II is simply a manifestation of another, irremissive battle. This conviction underpins the scene in which we encounter Nicholas for the first time, and in which, by quoting from Cavafy's "Expecting the Barbarians," Spark shows how in peacetime barbarianism has been assimilated by the very people who have been opposing it, and how the physical battle of the war has now become interiorized as a psychomachia. Here is a paragraph of the poem not quoted by the author, but relevant none the less:

> Because night is here but the barbarians have not come.
> Some people arrived from the frontiers,
> and they said that there are no longer any barbarians.[9]

This is the undertow beneath all the indulgent and affectionate nostalgia with which the girls are treated. Spark generally relays their preoccupations without comment, allowing her own attitudes to emerge through inserted scenes and interlaced quotation, most of the latter deriving from Joanna's speech lessons. Indeed, Jay L. Halio has gone so far as to say that the "most arresting aspect of this novel . . . is the way poetry interleaves through it . . . highlighting and commenting upon both the characters and the action."[10] Even so, glints of irony do become apparent in various inflections of the prose, as in the use of "vital" to describe the dormitory obsessions with love and money. The juxtaposition is damning enough to begin

---

8. *Passion and Society*, 45.
9. C. P. Cavafy, *The Complete Poems of Cavafy*, 19.
10. "Muriel Spark: The Novelist's Sense of Wonder," 272.

with, and we do not have to read much further to discover that the love that they discuss is nothing more than an adolescent version of eros. Its dubious nature is especially apparent in the way the girls define it by the ancillaries of "looks" and "money." In fact no one in the entire hostel has anything like a satisfactory conception of love. This is not only because the girls are all immature—the boarding house has a hierarchy of age and experience that corresponds with its architectural levels, and on some of these are grown women. In the dormitory is the undifferentiated mass of the young girls, characterized by the unison of their responses and by an image of flocking birds that points their lack of individuation. On the level above them are the celibates, who are also dealt with collectively to point the analogue between the unawakened sexuality of the girls below them and their own. It is on this level that Joanna significantly has her room, occupying, as she does, a medial position between these two groups. Above her in turn are five other named participants around whom the narrative turns. Manipulation and worldliness characterize this terrace of the mock-purgatorial mountain, which exits into a heaven of social glamour. We are informed that three of them, while they sleep with men, withhold their favors from those they intend to marry.

If Joanna's Romantic excessiveness has led her to a false vocation, her idealism is still to be preferred to the superficiality of Selina and her circle. Surface, not spirit, provides the measure of excellence at this level, as witness its obsession with diet, ironically counterpointed against Joanna's with poetry. We must bear in mind the climax of the book, in which the worldly "grace" of a slim figure becomes a means of "salvation." Only the slim girls are able to wriggle through the lavatory window and so escape the fire when it breaks out. Selina is the most glamorous of these. She proves the spiritual successor to Hans Andersen's Karen, the girl who trod on a loaf, and similarly subordinates the claims of humanity to those of appearance. When she is introduced to Nicholas Farringdon, her body is comically seen to have a self-awareness so developed as to dispose itself to advantage without the intervention of her mind (p. 49). Her body and soul, by implication, are equivalent. The former has to be tutored and disciplined in grace, but the grace of deportment and composure, not the theological kind.

At times that blasphemously approximate those of the Angelus, Selina recites a creed that celebrates her own incarnation: "The Two Sentences were a simple morning and evening exercise prescribed by the Chief Instructress of the Poise Course which Selina had recently taken, by correspondence, in twelve lessons for five guineas. . . . Poise is perfect balance, an equanimity of body and mind, complete composure whatever the social scene" (pp. 59–60). This travesty of stoic ataraxia obviously lays the foundation for her retrieval of the evening dress just before Joanna's death. Selina's vocation is a vocation of service to the self—and Dorothy and Anne exemplify the same tendency, though to a degree less extreme. Jane Wright, for all the muddle of her mind, is a rather more sympathetic figure because she at least is vulnerable, having failed to construct a shell of "poise" around her feelings. Even she, however, is not without pretentiousness. This takes the form of masking her humdrum job with glamorous phrases, so that she refers with a mechanical insistence straight out of Bergson to "the world of books" and to "brainwaves," one of which prompts her to write to Henry James in 1945! Her structural function in the book is that of *ficelle*—it is through her repeated telephone calls to her contemporaries at the May of Teck Club that we are able to gauge their damning continuity with their former selves—and she is also instrumental in introducing Nicholas Farringdon to the hostel.

The author stresses the uncentered nature of Nicholas's life before this and his dilettantish trifling with identities. In the light of his uncertainty, his eventual conversion becomes, like Ronald's submission to his epilepsy, a conferral of purpose:

> From Rudi she gathered that before the war he had always been undecided whether to live in England or France, and whether he preferred men or women, since he alternated between passionate intervals with both. Also, he could never make up his mind between suicide and an equally drastic course of action known as Father D'Arcy. Rudi explained that the latter was a Jesuit philosopher who had the monopoly for converting the English intellectuals. (p. 63)

Velma Richmond has pointed out that "divine Grace comes 'involuntarily,' not by seeking."[11] Although this claim overlooks the case of Caroline Rose in *The Comforters*, who, like Spark herself, has reached religious conviction by force of reason, it does apply to the operation of grace in Nicholas's conversion. For this turns not on an act of will—his toying with decisions of identity makes that much clear—but on an *involuntary* signature of the cross.

A randomness in Nicholas's unpublished *Sabbath Notebooks* reveals that his writing has been as unpurposed as his life before

11. *Muriel Spark*, 89.

that moment of grace. While Rudi (Jane Wright's friend) subjects the notebooks to dismissive analysis, she is swept up in speculations about the life that has brought them to birth. The intrusive sounds of piano and Joanna's declamation add further voices to a fugue of disconnections in this masterly part of the novel. Rudi reads an extract from *The Sabbath Notebooks* in which Nicholas presents anarchism not as a political theory but as something as central to human existence as the physiology of the heart. The argument is not developed or worked through, but simply presented as a thought, which is Nicholas's format for the entire book. This preference for *pensée* above discourse tends to align him with the author, whose art of compression also fights shy of discursive prose. Another point of contact between them is the way in which Nicholas keeps returning to theological ideas, though his treatment of them is more secular than reverent. Rudi is quick to point out that this has brought him into disrepute with more committed anarchists, for even within a context of formal anarchy Nicholas tends to be anarchical, failing to speak the dialect expected of him. The thrust behind his epigram about anarchism and the heartbeat is therefore crypto-religious: rebellion against order is as old as *non serviam*, and as central to human experience as the bloodstream. The corollary, though this is not stated, is that only by acknowledging and submitting to that order can humankind find vocation. An echo of Ecclesiastes ("there is no new thing under the sun," 1:9) in Nicholas's claim that anarchism is nothing new of itself brings to mind the preacher's cry of vanity, and also gives his cynicism a religious color. Thus Spark to some extent prepares for his eventual conversion, though its suddenness and unpredictability are still stressed as the features of inscrutable grace. Nicholas might be confused and incapable of sustained thought, but the positive side of this negative perception is that he is open-minded and receptive to change. Already he seems to realize that if the human will provides the ordering principle instead of the divine, disorder results. All that remains for him to do is to conform that will to God's. Rudi is a foreigner and speaks English with many faults of idiom and other mannerisms. One of these is the functionless repetition of "by the way"; the phrase suddenly lights up with thematic relevance, however, when it is put alongside an observation about Nicholas's diversionism. We are reminded of Isaiah's sheep and the willfulness of a humankind "turned every one to his own way." The oscillations and undirectedness of Nicholas's life can also be explained in these terms. And so too his failure to sustain anything, which his

preference for aphorism attests. Yet there is real aspiration behind
this muddle, an aspiration that the quotation from Blake, entering
into the polyphonic texture of the passage by way of Joanna's speech
lesson, helps bring into focus:

> Ah! Sun-flower! weary of time,
> Who countest the steps of the Sun;
> Seeking after that sweet golden clime,
> Where the traveller's journey is done;

"Now try it," said Joanna. "Very slowly on the third line. Think of a
sweet golden clime as you say it."

> Ah! Sun-flower! . . .

The dormitory girls who had spilled out of the drawing room on to
the terrace chattered like a parliament of fowls. The little notes of the
scales followed one another obediently. (p. 68)

That this is immensely skillful and poignant writing it goes without saying. The possibility that the Blake might strike too full a note
is kept in check by the domestic realities in the background—"an
elocution lesson with Miss Harper, the cook, in the half-hour before
the Sunday joint was ready to go in the oven" (p. 68)—and the
matter-of-fact way in which Joanna reduces the paradisal absolute
of "that sweet golden clime" to any old one that comes to mind.
Blake's golden clime is the world of prelapsarian perfection that
Nicholas projects upon the boarding house, which, for Jane and her
friends, remains precisely that—a prosaic boarding house. "Weariness of time" has caused his protean shifts of personality and identity and has given him mature individuation against the adolescent
mass of girls who enter here, the medieval meaning of "foules"
replaced by the unglamorous twentieth-century one. Their conformity and mass behavior is further imaged in the ordered sequence
of scales, which Spark seems to have borrowed from MacNeice's
sonnet about a Sunday morning. Scales are harmonic rough materials that have still to be transformed into music. But the effect of
the whole scene is less portentous than my analysis has made it out
to be. The touch is very light. While Rudi's account of The Sabbath
Notebooks is filling in the background to Nicholas's vocation, Jane,
bored by abstract thought, is sifting the details of his personal life,
as if in preparation for her later job as a gossip columnist.

Just as in The Bachelors the narrator reverts halfway through to
the impersonal, panoramic mode of the opening, so in The Girls of
Slender Means she makes use of a comparable Verfremdungseffek,
inverting the telescope upon the scene she has just managed so

deftly and movingly in close-up, and proceeding with unsentimental dispatch into the future to draw a line between Nicholas before and Nicholas after the turning point:

> So much for the portrait of the martyr as a young man as it was suggested to Jane on a Sunday morning between armistice and armistice, in the days of everyone's poverty, in 1945. . . .
> Meantime, Nicholas touched lightly on the imagination of the girls of slender means, and they on his. He had not yet slept on the roof with Selina on the hot summer nights . . . and he had not yet witnessed that action of savagery so extreme that it forced him involuntarily to make an entirely unaccustomed gesture, the signing of the cross upon himself. (pp. 72–73)

By now the sprightly aphorism about niceness and poverty has lost some of its bounce, and the spiritual as well as the material impoverishment of the city is hinted by "everyone's poverty." In a way that travesties the reverent tone of Catholic hagiography, Spark changes gear at the phrase "So much for the portrait of the martyr," which, by perfunctorily displacing "artist" with "martyr," also passes judgment on Nicholas's aspirations as a writer. Her tone makes it clear that these have little meaning in themselves; it is only as background to the conversion (proleptically suggested by the substitution of "martyr" for "artist") that they take on value. The chapter ends with Jane's informing Rudi of Nicholas's death over the telephone. A bad line makes for bathos—and in the stop and start of the exchange, Spark alludes once again to Auden's "Musée des Beaux Arts" and even, perhaps, to Keats's "Ode on a Grecian Urn." *Market* in the rural sense gives way to *market* in the capitalist, and, with a stroke of irony, Nicholas's work becomes a material commodity at the very moment his spiritual stature has been confirmed:

> ". . . a hut . . ."
> "I can't hear . . ."
> ". . . in a valley . . ."
> "Speak loud."
> ". . . in a clump of palms . . . deserted . . . it was market day, everyone had gone to market."
> "I find it. There is maybe a market for this Sabbath book." (p. 86)

The protean *Sabbath Notebooks* have in Rudi's memory lost their plural and taken on the radiant absoluteness of Scripture, their once anarchic use of a Christian term somehow turned to piety. But all this is paradoxically devalued by Rudi's materialistic valuation of the manuscript.

Chapter 5, like Chapter 4, is given over to an extended scene in the May of Teck Club, both statically "atmospheric" and dynamically concerned with advancing the friendship between Nicholas and Selina. The time, as before, is Sunday morning, appropriate enough for the compiler of *Sabbath Notebooks*. This recurring use of Sunday suggests that grace has begun to forge a pattern where none before has existed. Sundays have only a secular meaning for the hostel, and yet on each occasion Nicholas is slowly being led toward his destiny. The unlikely guide for this is Selina, dressed in a fashion claiming inspiration from the Resistance. This is yet another variation on the idea of symbols made meaningless by disconnection. High-brimmed hats and wedge shoes have no organic connection with the heroism they claim to represent, and May of Teck Sundays by the same token have little connection with religious sabbaths, symbols of redeemed time. Yet all the while the time *is* being redeemed, and the groundwork for Nicholas's conversion being prepared. With him is a guest from a branch of American Intelligence, who is also Selina's lover, but whose difference of character creates one of the Sparkian diptychs that sharpen her portraiture through a systematic use of contrast—we have already seen the contrastive coupling of Seton and Ronald in *The Bachelors*, for example. Just as the worldly nature of Selina is set off by Joanna's Romantic selflessness, so Nicholas's "anarchic" indifference to form registers against the tentative chivalry of the American, who half gets out of his chair every time one of the girls dances attendance on him. (Nicholas, by contrast, is presented as sprawling in his like a nobleman of the ancien régime.) Yet, although the difference between the two men is vast, Nicholas perceives a similarity in the way they both respond to the boarding house. Although he would like to see himself standing for realism, and the colonel for the unrealities of romance, it is clear to him that both have been guilty of idealizing the girls: "The Colonel seemed to be in love with the entire club, Selina being the centre and practical focus of his feelings in this respect. This was a common effect of the May of Teck Club on its male visitors . . ." (pp. 88–89). In a moment of recognition, Nicholas perceives that he too has been imposing imagery upon the girls, not observing them. And here too lies the weakness of his political theorizing in the *Notebooks*, which also lacks empirical ground. Its way of formulating thought in "poetic" *pensées* (not in logical discourse) points to its status as an imaginative rather than a sociological construct. Equally "poetic" is the divorce of theory from fact, whether in the *Notebooks* or in the May of Teck, because, as in the case of Joanna's sterile resolve, it imposes a pattern that has no foundation in fact. The imposition "upon this little society [of an] image incomprehensible to itself" (p. 89) provides an index to the weakness of Nicholas's social speculations. These, presenting anarchic guesses as prophetically final truths, amount to that *giving* of a discussion that so amuses him in the warden's announcement about a visit from the Tory M.P. But, even though they are not quite as imperious as that, the *Sabbath Notebooks* also in a sense offer a preelection discussion, if we take *election* to refer to Nicholas's response to a calling.

Their ferment is proof at least of the vital spirit that Felix Dobell fails to command, something emphasized by the Absurdist conversation between the two men. Nicholas, holding forth as an anarchist about the undesirability of central government, is startled to be told that the colonel's wife belongs to the Guild of Ethical Guardians. He is baffled by the non sequitur until he realizes that Dobell has perceived him to be an idealist and, knowing his wife to have ideals as well, has used that common denominator to connect an anarchist preaching licence and chaos with a prudish censor. (Gareth Dobell rubberstamps magazines and books that have been approved by the guild for use in the home.) This Beckettian comedy is delightful in itself, but it also shows how Felix simply embraces the axioms that Nicholas in his endless searching and experimenting has tried to understand. The author leaves no doubt which option is more likely to open itself to the workings of grace. And even though Nicholas might pontificate and preen himself on his *pensées*, he is shown to have a tact and kindness that resembles Ronald's in *The Bachelors*. Whereas one imagines that most self-respecting anarchists would laugh rudely in the face of a man as obtuse as the colonel, Nicholas shows himself to be a mock-respectful student of Selina's "poise," suppressing ridicule for politeness, self-advancement for consideration of the other. Selina, watching this strange encounter from the sidelines, becomes aware that Nicholas is too odd to be socially acceptable and considers ways of exploiting his eccentricity to her own advantage. And Jane, rather more intelligent, and vexed by the confusion, tries to explain to Felix that Nicholas *is* an anarchist, to which he responds with good-natured incredulity, vaguely aware that anarchists are not altogether "clubbable."

Balance is the key here as elsewhere in Spark, balance not only as it is reflected in Nicholas's amiable version of "poise," but also as it relates to the fusing of extremes—Dobell's placid practicality and the idealism that Nicholas has shown in the *Sabbath Notebooks*. As

Nicholas has dwelt too exclusively in the sphere of theory, so has Felix been guilty of the opposite in delegating his moral and his mental life to his wife. Gareth Dobell has in fact become the embodiment of her husband's conscience and has superstitiously to be held at bay with lock and key every time he commits adultery with Selina. This abjectness is something that Selina, for whom poise is self-sufficiency, cannot understand, although it is proof at least of a *sense* of sin. Selina's poise is utterly amoral and utterly self-absorbed. It is presented later in the same scene as the apparently superhuman disposition of events to its own advantage, its effortlessness the mask of a ruthless will. Jane, a disaffected spectator, knows in advance that Selina will somehow arrange the outing to her own benefit and secure a back seat with Nicholas while Jane and the colonel occupy the front of the car.

Where Selina is in focus, Joanna is often to be found alongside, and the sabbath scene ends with a conversation between Felix and Nicholas that never took place, but that is nonetheless reified as an entry in the *Sabbath Notebooks*. It is now becoming clear that this manuscript will form the *liber scriptus* of a martyr's conversion, a conversion delicately prophesied by the "holy dread" and "milk of paradise" of the poem Joanna is intoning:

> Nicholas almost said, "She is orgiastical in her feeling for poetry. I can hear it in her voice," but refrained in case the Colonel should say "Really?" and he should go on to say, "Poetry takes the place of sex for her, I think."
>
> "Really? She looked sexually fine to me."
>
> Which conversation did not take place, and Nicholas kept it for his notebooks. (p. 101)

The parallel between this spectral conversation and the empty church in which Joanna and her father recite the psalms helps connect Nicholas with Joanna, since it is only by virtue of a greater consciousness that both utterances become real in the Berkeleyan sense. Father and daughter recite the Anglican cycle of psalms "as it seemed to the empty pews, but by faith to the congregations of the angels, the Englishly rendered intentions of the sweet singer of Israel" (pp. 104–5). Neither the recitations of Joanna and her father nor the conversation of Nicholas with the colonel is any the less valid for having no tangible audience.

The interrelatedness of Selina and Joanna as antagonists of evil and good becomes more and more apparent as the story unfolds, and the parallel between the microcosm of the club and the state of the world leads Nicholas to invest it with a sort of miniature *anima mundi*:

> The sounds and sights impinging on him from the hall of the club intensified themselves, whenever he called, into one sensation, as if with a will of their own. He thought of the lines:
>
>> *Let us roll all our strength, and all*
>> *Our sweetness up into one ball;*
>
> And I would like, he thought, to teach Joanna that poem or rather demonstrate it; and he made spasmodic notes on the back pages of his *Sabbath* manuscript. (p. 106)

The irony, of course, is to be found in the fact that it is Joanna who demonstrates the collection and exercise of strength to Nicholas, substituting a spiritual seduction for his intended sexual one. Marian imagery later confirms her role as a mediator of grace: "Joanna needs to know more of life, thought Nicholas, as he loitered in the hall on one specific evening, but if she knew life she would not be proclaiming these words so sexually and matriarchally as if in the ecstatic act of suckling a divine child" (p. 108).

At this point the voice of Winston Churchill is reproduced in unison by all the wireless sets of the hostel—as the stampede is multiplied on the television sets in Lise's department store—and parallels Joanna's intemperate choice (her election to a life of poetry) with the preelection rhetoric of a politician. She falls silent in deference to its empty jeremiad:

> Nicholas imagined Joanna standing by her bed, put out of business as it were, but listening, drawing it into her bloodstream. As in a dream of his own that depicted a dream of hers, he thought of Joanna in this immovable attitude, given up to the cadences of the wireless as if it did not matter what was producing them, the politician or herself. She was a proclaiming statue in his mind.
>
> A girl in a long evening dress slid in the doorway, furtively. Her hair fell round her shoulders in a brown curl. Through the bemused mind of the loitering, listening man went the fact of a girl slipping furtively into the hall; she had a meaning, even if she had no meaningful intention. (p. 110)

In the light of the Labour victory in the election that follows the events of the novel, Churchill's rhetoric seems impotent and foredoomed. Joanna, Nicholas imagines, must be drawing the plangent but meaningless tirade into her bloodstream. Her life, too, has been reduced to vocal expertise. Of course the image of her drinking in the rhetoric is colored by his preconceptions, and has no more reality than his nonconversation with Felix Dobell, but it is a just one, especially since the Galatea-like metaphor of the statue points to the girl's underdeveloped emotional life. She will never be vitalized by Nicholas/Pygmalion, but she will paradoxically vitalize him in turn, and her proclamation will become not the quivering delivery of a rhetorician, but a statement of faith. In dying, Joanna will become the icon of a virgin martyr.

At this point Spark introduces Pauline Fox, the mad girl whose life centers on imaginary dinners with a film star. We shift from the marmoreal, white fixity of Joanna, conceived as a proclaiming statue, to someone with an apparently vital presence ("Her hair fell round her shoulder in a brown curl"), but find that she is actually more spectral, more prone than Joanna herself to substitute Romantic figment for reality. She enters the narrative as an epistemological datum, not as a character in her own right. Her life of fantasy is meaningless, but, as a corrective image of fantasy gone astray, she has meaning. Meaning is conferred by the plot, not by herself, just as Joanna's meaning derives from an inscrutable divine economy, not from the choices she has consciously made to reach her present position.

All of which bears on the theme of vocation and identity, on the revelatory crisis to which the novel is moving all the time. Already we see Nicholas directing perceptions of fact against a fantasy, which, like Lamia's in the poem by Keats, cannot withstand them:

> It [the dress] was colored dark blue, green, orange and white in a floral pattern as from the Pacific Islands.
>   He said, "I don't think I've ever seen such a gorgeous dress."
>   "Schiaparelli," she said.
>   He said, "Is it the one you swap among yourselves?"
>   "Who told you that?"
>   "You look beautiful," he replied.
>   She picked up the rustling skirt and floated away up the staircase.
>   Oh, girls of slender means!
>   The election speech having come to an end, everybody's wireless was turned off for a space, as if in reverence to what had just passed through the air. (pp. 112–13)

The dress's Pacific Island vividness hints, perhaps, at its instrumental role in the events that will lead to Nicholas's martyrdom in a different tropical setting. Its exotic brilliance in any event provides an emblem of life far removed from the austerities of the May of Teck Club, another displacement of reality by romance. Pauline

Fox's fictive dinners with a film star are a version of the unreality that, at the other end of its range, takes the form of Joanna's Petrarchan idealism, and her entry here is strategic. So too is her failure to answer Nicholas when he asks her about the dress-swapping, meeting a demand for truth with illusory levitation—"and floated away up the staircase." Pauline has as little substance as the rhetoric that, also impalpable, has "just passed through the air."

Into this strange world of phantasms and figments comes the figure of Selina, no less insubstantial in her solipsism. (One wonders, indeed, whether the author had Thomas Gray's Selima in mind when she named her.) That integration of body and spirit, of soul and matter, which in Spark's scheme of things signifies psychic health, is nowhere to be found. As a result, there is a surreal interchangeability between these disembodied voices and dresses that are drifting in and out of Nicholas's consciousness:

> Selina came down presently. Poise is perfect balance, an equanimity of body and mind. Down the staircase she floated, as it were even more realistically than had the sad communer with the spirit of Jack Buchanan a few moments ago floated up it. It might have been the same girl, floating upwards in a Schiaparelli rustle of silk with a shining hood of hair, and floating downwards in a slim skirt with a white-spotted blue blouse, her hair now piled high. (pp. 113–14)

Selina's hard-nosed resolve to pursue her own advantage would at first seem to distinguish her from Pauline Fox, to give her a reality, however crude. And yet, even though she is seen to float down "realistically," a subjunctive phrase converts that realistic descent into illusion as well. As in her great aside about eternal life in *The Takeover*, Spark seems bent on subordinating the tangible reality of the boarding house to the intangible reality of the events that are soon to occur on its blazing rooftop. The stanza from Poe's "To One in Paradise," sounding from Joanna's room at this point, helps re-project the prelapsarian innocence that Nicholas has imposed upon the hostel, its Romantic falsity similarly pointed by the image of a trance. Like Joanna's curate, he has still to be tempered by immersion in the real:

"Good evening," said Nicholas.

> And all my days are trances,
> And all my nightly dreams
> And where thy dark eye glances,
> And where thy footstep gleams—

> In *what ethereal dances,*
> *By what eternal streams!*

"Now repeat," said Joanna's voice.
"Come on then," said Selina . . . . (p. 114)

The fact that it is only Joanna's voice that we hear makes her seem incorporeal, and, in the context of the poem and its title, its bodilessness seems also to foreshadow her death. While Nicholas is thinking of a paradisal *locus amoenus*, she is pointing to a celestial paradise. The lesson she presents is one that he cannot at this stage get by heart because Selina is beckoning him on to passion.

Nicholas's courtship of Selina is educative as well as passionate, for he tries to fill the vacant symbol of the girl with the significance he feels she ought to have, to connect the semblance of humanity to real human feeling. But, since he is for the time being caught up in an idealism that makes for a comparable unreality, the effort is foredoomed:

> With the reckless ambition of a visionary, he pushed his passion for Selina into a desire that she, too, should accept and exploit the outlines of poverty in her life. He loved her as he loved his native country. He wanted Selina to be an ideal society personified amongst her bones, he wanted her beautiful limbs to obey her mind and heart like intelligent men and women, and for these to possess the same grace and beauty as her body. Whereas Selina's desires were comparatively humble, she only wanted, at that particular moment, a packet of hairgrips which had just then disappeared from the shops for a few weeks.
>
> It was not the first instance of a man taking a girl to bed with the aim of converting her soul, but he, in great exasperation, felt that it was, and poignantly, in bed, willed and willed the awakening of her social conscience. . . . It was incredible to him that she should not share with him an understanding of the lovely attributes of dispossession and poverty, her body was so austere and economically furnished. (pp. 116–17)

The recklessness with which Nicholas here confounds theoretical desiderata and physical desire points, as in the case of the *Sabbath Notebooks,* to a disregard for reality, a forcing of truth into the mould of preconception. So intensely is the theory held that theoretical "wants" come to displace or compete with sexual appetite. He projects a symbolic vision upon the reality of Selina, who is otherwise thinking prosaically of hair-grips. It is an order of relationship that, for all its evidence of physical satisfaction, resembles Joanna's high-flown celibacy, except that it is the obsession with self (not self-oblation) that causes the unreality here. Eros of its very nature cannot be converted by an act of will into agape.

Although Nicholas feels shock at the superficial nature of the May of Teck romances, based as they are on the economic principle of exchange, he himself loves the hostel in a similar way. His affection is equally "economical" in its generality, and it is based not on real individuals, but on the symbolic denominator he perceives to link them. The cheapness of life that has become a habitual assumption of the war years has led to a state of affairs in which commitment and the mourning it would ordinarily entail have become unaffordable luxuries. Promiscuity is in fact practiced in the belief that death, like the fiend in the choric simile from *The Ancient Mariner*, is stalking behind, and the thought of death, without a vocational framework to shape one's life, can be excluded only by company—any company. The replacement lover is significantly described as a "type." No name and identity are supplied:

> Nicholas, who was past his youth, was shocked at heart by their week-by-week emotions.
> "I thought you said she was in love with the boy."
> "So she was."
> "Well, wasn't it only last week that he died? You said he died of dysentery in Burma."
> "Yes I know. But she met this naval type on Monday, she's madly in love with him."
> "She can't be in love with him," said Nicholas.
> "Well, they've got a lot in common, she says."
> "A lot in common? It's only Wednesday now."
>
> > Like one, that on a lonesome road
> > Doth walk in fear and dread,
> > And having once turned round, walks on,
> > And turns no more his head;
> > Because he knows a frightful fiend
> > Doth close behind him tread. (p. 121)

The speaker is not identified in this exchange, but her unruffled "poise" gives us a clue as to who she might be.

The climactic chapter of the novel begins unnervingly with a false alarm, an unspecified scream of panic. This is followed by an assurance to the effect that at the May of Teck, screams were uttered frequently and could greet a funny joke or a mishap with a stocking. The narrator thus sets our minds at rest only to harrow them the more intensely when the actual disaster occurs. This rhythm of reassurance and violent disruption resembles the descriptive procedure in Chapter 1, though it is taken to an extreme here. Indeed Spark sometimes runs the risk of approximating the mode of the Calvinist God in this aspect of her narrative design—a mode that so horrifies Sandy in *The Prime of Miss Jean Brodie*:

> In some ways the most real and rooted people Sandy knew were Miss Gaunt and the Kerr sisters who made no evasions about their belief that God had planned for practically everybody before they were born a nasty surprise when they died. Later, when Sandy read John Calvin, she found that although the popular conceptions of Calvinism were sometimes mistaken, in this particular there was no mistake, indeed it was but a mild misunderstanding of the case, he having made it God's pleasure to implant in certain people an erroneous sense of joy and salvation, so that their surprise in the end might be the nastier.[12]

While the technique is taken to an intolerable extreme in *The Driver's Seat* and *Not to Disturb*, it has only a limited place in *The Girls of Slender Means*. The scream is premonitory—a visitor has become stuck in the fateful window as though in dress rehearsal for the events to come. Already we see Selina unruffled by the commotion, practicing her poise of uncompassion at the hour of the Angelus:

> "Just on six," said Anne.
> Selina looked at her watch to see if this was so, then walked towards her room.
> "Don't leave her, I'm getting help," Jane said.
> Selina opened the door of her room, but Anne stood gripping Tilly's ankles. As Jane reached the next landing she heard Selina's voice:
> "Poise is perfect balance, an equanimity . . . ." (p. 140)

Perhaps we are meant to recollect Cloe in Pope's *Epistle to a Lady* when we read this account of Selina—"She, while her Lover pants upon her breast, / Can mark the figures on an Indian chest." The converse of her mantra is Joanna's recitation of the *Ode to the West Wind*, with its stress on prophecy and self-renewal. Hearing the two in quick succession, Jane experiences an epiphany of innocence and corruption, of paradise and exile in the *vallis lacrimarum*:

> Jane was suddenly overcome by a deep envy of Joanna, the source of which she could not locate exactly at that hour of her youth. The feeling was connected with an inner knowledge of Joanna's disinterestedness, her ability, a gift, to forget herself and her personality.

12. Spark, *The Prime of Miss Jean Brodie*, 144–45. Henceforth cited parenthetically in the text by page number.

Jane suddenly felt miserable, as one who has been cast out of Eden before realising that it had in fact been Eden. (pp. 142–43)

She is also to learn from Nicholas that the experience of hell inheres less in the actual fire than in some of the responses it brings to light, though we are not given any indication that the lesson carries home:

"Yes, but she's [Selina] suffering from shock. I must have brought all the horrors back to her mind."
"It was hell," Jane said.
"I know." (pp. 179–80)

That the explosion and fire occur *sub specie aeternitatis* can be gauged from the way time and place are experienced by those in danger. Whereas the spectators are acutely aware of time as the catastrophe approaches, the victims experience the timelessness of suspension and detachment—they are compared anachronistically to space travellers who, exempt from time and gravity, have lost all connection with Earth. Spark locates them in 1945, and at the same time takes them out of that temporal context into the eternity of the Four Last Things. The novel began by looking back to 1945 as to a Romantic never-never; now it looks forward from that same year into an eschatological future. The eternal present of "The Solitary Reaper" is recalled when Spark speaks of time as a far-forgotten event: "old, unhappy far-off things, / And battles long ago." Joanna, living in the cyclical time of the liturgy, and declaiming the psalms appointed for Day 27 as she dies, will leave, like the solitary reaper on the poet's, an indelible impression on Nicholas's heart.

If time is a source of anxiety to the onlookers, there are others passing by to whom the events in the hostel have no meaning. It is true that the workers in the park do not turn away as in the Auden poem, but it is also true that their engagement does not extend beyond a faint curiosity. There is no *intersection* of time and eternity such as Eliot describes, only their juxtaposition:

As if hypnotised, they surrounded Joanna, and she herself stood as one hypnotised into the strange utterances of Day 27 in the Anglican order, held to be applicable to all sorts and conditions of human life in the world at that particular moment, when in London homing workers plodded across the Park, observing with curiosity the fire-engines in the distance, when Rudi Bittesch was sitting in his flat at St. John's Wood trying, without success, to telephone to Jane to speak to her privately, the Labour Government was new-born, and elsewhere on the face of the globe people slept, queued for liberation-rations, beat

the tom-toms, took shelter from the bombers or went for a ride on a
dodgem at the fun-fair. (pp. 162–63)

The point of this catalog is to suggest an unpatterned mass of events
both trivial and global, all "meaninglessly" synchronized with the
dark, providential death of Joanna. "Homing workers" who plod
across the park are faded contemporary epigones of Gray's plough-
man. They bring the *Elegy*'s contrast of philosophic vigilance and
unthinking exhaustion to mind. At the same time the mock-violent
leisure of a funfair is counterpointed with the terror that American
bombers hold for Japan—Hiroshima, after all, is a mere ten days
away. In the words of David Lodge, "Mrs. Spark denies solipsism
and posits some divine providence at work in the world; but this
providence remains ultimately mysterious and incomprehensible
because the world is a fallen one and not even the novelist can
understand it fully."[13] Yet even if the meaning of the cataclysm
cannot be grasped in all its fullness, its importance cannot be denied.

At the same time as it abolishes the categories of time and space
to let in a vision of eternity, the explosion is anticipated with a
scrupulous deference to the clock. The solemn anadiplosis that
straddles the paragraph break below reminds us that six o'clock is
the time set for Selina's recitation of her poise formula:

> Jane laughed foolishly to herself and descended to the telephone
> boxes as the clock in the hall struck six o' clock.
>
> *   *   *
>
> It struck six o' clock on that evening of July 27th. Nicholas has just
> returned to his room. (p. 140)

The deictic in "that evening" rings the date as on some calendar of
feast days, for it will be the most important in the life of the man
who has just returned to his room as casually as others are riding
dodgem cars or queuing for food. Time is about to be dismantled,
but at a point in time.

In the account of the fire itself, Spark for the last time plays
Romantic and realistic perceptions against each other. Nicholas's
first impression of Selina in the midst of the smoke is of someone
concerned for the welfare of others. He sees her refuse one of the
blankets being handed to the victims, even though she is barefoot
and clothed only in her underwear. This of course is the image of
the seductress in Wyatt's "They flee from me"—"With naked foot

13. "The Uses and Abuses of Omniscience: Method and Meaning in Muriel
Spark's *The Prime of Miss Jean Brodie*," 238.

stalking in my chamber"—but Nicholas chooses to see her rather as a vulnerable roe deer. Later he has to acknowledge the faultiness of his judgment:

> . . . she said, "Is it safe out here?" and at the same time was inspecting the condition of her salvaged item. Poise is perfect balance. It was the Schiaparelli dress. The coat-hanger dangled from the dress like a headless neck and shoulders.
> "Is it safe out here?" said Selina.
> "Nowhere's safe," said Nicholas. (pp. 160–61)

The incredulity that Nicholas feels is mimed here in the short, disconnected sentences, where in the interval between Selina's repeated questions, the disparate facts come together in his consciousness, and the coat-hanger becomes an emblem in its headless inhumanity of the dress's new and illegitimate owner.

Laced into the apparently banal exchange is a reference to the *Dies Irae*:

> *Quid sum miser tunc dicturus?*
> *Quem patronum rogaturus,*
> *Cum vix justus sit securus.*

Only in a godless or dualistic conception of the world can physical and spiritual security be divorced. Whereas Joanna is shown to have had a sense of hell (p. 171), Selina, passing through the fire unscathed to retrieve the dress, is revealed as being native and endued unto that element. She incarnates not the ideal society that Nicholas has forged from the emblem of her body, not the heavenly city of selfless sharing, but rather the selfishness of pandemonium itself. As Allan Casson puts it, "the crucial events leading to Nicholas's conversion are his visions of the 'hurtle of hell'—the public stabbing, and a beautiful young girl carrying a Schiaparelli dress."[14] The final jotting in the *Sabbath Notebooks* is a statement to the effect that "a vision of evil may be as effective to conversion as a vision of good" (p. 180). Its vision is compounded when, during the VJ celebrations, Nicholas sees a death occur with a nightmarish deletion of sound, and a sailor gratuitously stabs a woman in the midst of the rejoicing. In an emblematic gesture designed to acknowledge the ubiquity of evil, the fact that *vix justus sit securus*, he transfers a letter he has forged to the murderer's person, seeing a continuity between its untruthfulness and the greater crime. In

14. "Muriel Spark's *The Girls of Slender Means*," 96.

much the same way, Selina's salvage is related to the greater horrors of 1945. The hair-grips of that heartless girl haunt the last image of the book. Here, as if to confirm the interchangeability of the girls in the false vision of innocence, it is on Jane, barefoot like Selina in the fire, but sturdy as a peasant, that Spark freezes her final frame. Her preference for epigrammatic closure is apparent also in the way the last words balance the first in the novel, as though it were being bracketed in a massive *inclusio*:

> She had halted to pin up her straggling hair, and had a hair-pin in her mouth as she said it. Nicholas marvelled at her stamina, recalling her in this image years later in the country of his death—how she stood, sturdy and bare-legged on the dark grass, occupied with her hair—as if this was an image of all the May of Teck establishment in its meek, unselfconscious attitudes of poverty, long ago in 1945. (p. 183)

3

The Mandelbaum Gate
Integrative Vocation

Whereas Ronald Bridges has already found his vocation before the start of *The Bachelors* and strives always to secure its meaning in the face of existentialist despair, Nicholas Farringdon's inward life is documented near to the point of his calling, in the midst of his spiritual muddle. *The Mandelbaum Gate,* on the other hand, gives the topics of vocation and identity a different form in the dilemma of Barbara Vaughan. Two antagonistic demands on her soul, her Catholic faith and her attachment to a divorced man, compounded with the apparent antagonism of her Judaic and Gentile heritage, issue in bewildered stalling. This needs to be resolved before life can proceed with "meaningful intention," and the resolution—a protracted and passionate one—constitutes the chief theme of the novel.

Indeed it is in this that we can locate the difference between *The Mandelbaum Gate* and other Spark novels—its uncharacteristic obsessiveness. The author is clearly in control, but she makes that control less palpable than is customary with her, and she also uses monologic techniques to a greater degree than anywhere else in her fiction (if we leave aside such first-person narratives as *Robinson, Loitering with Intent,* and *A Far Cry from Kensington*). Her heroine, moreover, is uncharacteristic in the store she sets by large emotion, by engagement and passionate conviction—tenets which put her apart from the dry reticence of Ronald, whom she otherwise resembles as a figure bent on the task of religious self-discovery. The chronology of the novel is likewise symptomatic of its difference, since it avoids the neat, commentative montage of future and present we find in *The Girls of Slender Means.* In its place is a restless assemblage—fragments of distant past, recent past, and an irresolute present that Barbara attempts to worry into focus. This narrative procedure applies not only to the passionate pilgrim who is the novel's heroine—Chapter 7 is named after Walter Raleigh's poem, and, as Velma Richmond has noted, "succinctly states the novel's theme"[1]—but also to Freddy, the diplomat who offsets her anguished, feeling choices with his lack of commitment.

The novel in fact opens inside his thoughts[2] as they trail along inconsequentially and randomly—a far cry from the epigrammatic disposition of material that we find in the exordia of other Spark books. Returning from a visit to Jordan (the frontier at the time of the novel passes through Jerusalem itself), Freddy tries to compose some society verse to thank his hostess for her hospitality. This is one of his customs. He takes complex, honorific lyric stanzas associated with the troubadours and with courtly love and makes them over into entertainments, as if to expiate for his dullness at the dinner table. By canalizing chitchat into rondeaux redoublés, villanelles, rondels, and Sicilian octaves, Freddy is draining passion from form and offering a social husk for what was once a kernel of feeling. His society verse, accommodated in its incongruent structures, is an image of himself, of an adaptability both amiable and trivial. Fearful of "offensive" individuality, he has made it his vocation to smooth and soothe, as becomes his diplomatic profession. The Catholic habit of spiritual recollection at the end of each day— Jean Taylor in *Memento Mori* is an example of a character who profits by the exercise—is reduced to a "penitential" survey of his visit, but it is trivialized in the manner of his troubadour pastiche. His thoughts center not on issues of conscience, but on lapses of social finesse: his conscience is pricked by his failure to say anything between the soup and the fish. Life for him has been devoted to deleting "notes" of personality, since it is in *differentiation* that the potentialities of conflict lie. He is actually quite right to perceive the connection between personal and public intercourse and to note how a tedious or an overwitty guest can cause disruption at the dinner table and ultimately even tension between nations. The point is whether the dinner table is a satisfactory norm for the course of human affairs. By making mere agreeableness his vocation, Freddy has dismantled his true personality and substituted one that is bland and synthetic. Indeed, like the Cheshire cat, he has distilled himself into the metonymy of a smile, the winning quality of which he has perfected even in babyhood.

1. *Muriel Spark,* 103.
2. Spark, *The Mandelbaum Gate,* 3ff. Henceforth cited parenthetically in the text by page number.

In Freddy's unindividual identity is the antitype of Barbara's search for meaning through the *integration,* not the suppression, of the self. The verse he composes must not seem effortful, since effort implies dedication, and dedication is too "extreme" for someone bent on maintaining untroubled surfaces—a version of *sprezzatura* as debased as his mock troubadour lyrics. Although the narrator herself suggests that there is an imaginative potentiality in Freddy that, with passion to activate it, might have made a poet of him, he remains a versifier manqué for want of that very passion.

As he ambles through the streets of the Orthodox Quarter in Jerusalem, he reduces to "absurdity" any sign of impassioned allegiance, whether it be national or cultural. The implicit yardsticks for these judgments are British good form, that debased (because inelastic) version of the *via media,* and the assumed superiority of British institutions. Freddy's ability to feel for others is thus impaired by a cultural arrogance that blocks off anything approaching empathy. He regards the Orthodox Jewish adolescents he passes as versions of the British schoolboy he himself was and assumes that their badges of separation—their ringlets, for example—must make life hell for them. His stock adjective, *absurd,* becomes a mock-Homeric epithet, to be dealt out indiscriminately to anything his prejudices prevent him from assimilating. Indeed, it even becomes a shibboleth without which he finds himself unable to start a friendship. A sense of the absurd is a corollary of detachment, and it is only with the detached that Freddy feels at ease. A man of limited responses, he turns the usual workings of empathy inside out and makes his own experience the measure of others'. We have already seen it in the way he uses medieval verse forms for the lightest sort of verse and in the way he reacts to the Orthodox adolescents. It is evident also in the way his sense of "hell" lacks all eschatological force and becomes the discomfort of a British schoolboy. Small wonder that he should come close to quarreling with Barbara when they first meet. Any version of religion that extends beyond a set of moral imperatives will necessarily prove "absurd" and extreme in his eyes.

Freddy's national complacency also trenches more than once on racism. If British institutions and British temperament are fetishized as exemplars of sanity, anything that differs from them must also be dismissed as "absurd." Even so contingent and irrelevant a datum as a dark skin color becomes for Freddy an emblem of intemperance to be measured by the "ideal" of English pallor (p. 5). In the same way, his apparently innocent concern with genealogy and family groupings shades into a far-from-innocent anti-Semitic distaste when he is recovering from the adventure in Jordan (p. 127). Irritated by the fact that the doctor examining him is called Jarvis, he asks himself how a Jew can come by a name that is the birthright of the English landed gentry and imagines that some alien Continental name like "Jarvinsky" must lie behind the "acceptable" English one.

Diplomatic life in a foreign country is by definition marginal, and while this marginality might be thought to confer perspective, it ought not to block any effort toward cultural understanding. Indeed, successful diplomats have to make at least some attempt to understand the culture in which their posting has been made. Of this, as we have seen, Freddy is temperamentally incapable. He might make a token stab at learning the language, but this is offset by his readiness to reduce foreign cultures to an aggregate of sense impressions (many of them dismissive) (p. 6). Furthermore, his cultivation of friends who share his complacency and his "temperateness" points to a failure to extend himself in challenging relationships. That he should choose to learn Arabic with Abdul Ramdez, detached and disaffected, is proof of this. In handling Freddy's Laodicean attitude, Spark departs from her usual procedure of ridicule. Ridicule works on the Freddyesque assumption that everything is potentially absurd, and in earlier and later fiction she often takes up this position to cool and dissociate our responses lest we lose our perspective through *Miteinfühlung*. This disavowal of the absurd in *The Mandelbaum Gate*, and the deeply felt quality that results from the disavowal, account in some measure for its being sui generis in a canon of novels that are otherwise distinctly unearnest. Intensity is not a quality that one seeks in the fiction of Muriel Spark, and yet it is intensity that is being endorsed implicitly in the satiric presentation of Freddy, and quite frontally in the characterization of Barbara Vaughan. Her quest for identity *is* to all intents and purposes her spiritual vocation. She stands for a feeling submission to, not the cautious skirting of, experience.

This much becomes apparent when the characters are brought together for the first time. Against the intensity Freddy ascribes to Barbara, Spark sets his vacant smile, which a possessive pronoun equates with his very selfhood. Indeed, he has earlier been shown to smile in benevolent acknowledgment of the fact that he has a smile. A friend of his later chatters on about the significance of smiles—after all, smiles are simply contractions of the facial muscles. Because her husband finds his emotions are affected by the nature of his smile, she wonders which determines which (p. 65). It is of course only when the signifier and signified are reversed in this way, or when the smile is hypostatized as an end in itself, that the tail can be said to wag the dog. The one that Freddy beams so cherubically at Barbara when first they meet is in any case masking a slight fear—his congenital fear of intensity.

> His first meeting with Miss Vaughan now came back . . . . His first impression had been of a pleasant English spinster; she was a teacher of English at a girls' school; she was on tour of the Holy Land . . . .
> Now, sitting with her near the same spot as when they had first spoken three weeks ago, he was filled with a sense of her dangerousness; he was obscurely afraid. (pp. 11–12)

One can see at first how pleased he is that Barbara seems to conform to pattern, a stereotype whose cultural familiarity impinges on the style as a tickable list of expectations—"she was a teacher of English at a girls' school; she was on a tour of the Holy Land." The moment she diverges from being English and "safe" (she is half-Jewish and is agonizing about contrary claims of passion and faith), she fills Freddy with a "sense of her dangerousness," which is to say, a sense of her unclassifiability. The encounter develops further:

> "Most of these Jews here are unbelievers, so far as I can gather."
> "Not quite," said Miss Vaughan, "I think they believe in a different way from what you mean. . . . Being a Jew isn't something they consider in their minds, weigh up, and give assent to as one does in the Western Christian tradition. Being a Jew is inherent."
> "Yes, I'm afraid so." Freddy gave a little laugh.
> As if he had not spoken at all, she continued. "As a half-Jew myself, I think I understand how—"
> "Oh, I didn't mean to say . . . I mean . . . One says things without thinking, you know."
> She said, "You might have said worse."
> Freddy felt terrible. He groped for the idea that, being a half-Jew, she might be only half-offended. (pp. 12–13)

Freddy's superficial conception of the country in which he is stationed declares itself in the way he underestimates not only Orthodox devoutness but also the cultural (as opposed to religious) aspects of Judaism. His generalization about unbelief in Israel might pass muster in the unconsidered chitchat of a cocktail party, but it hardly amounts to a considered truth. On the other hand, Barbara's response, with its impassioned, not to say Lawrentian avowal of blood-thought, would be inappropriate to the pleasantries of an embassy reception. This in itself is proof of the challenge she offers to Freddy's insular values, evident above all in the anti-Semitic remark he makes on the assumption that they are both inherently (and preferably) English. When he discovers his faux pas, he regrets it not so much because what he has said is untrue, but because he has been guilty of a professional failing—the art of diplomacy requires him to *conceal* illiberal thoughts, if not necessarily to root them out. That he takes his racist and other prejudicial attitudes to be held by sensible (British) people can be detected in the impersonal *one* to whom he ascribes the derogatory words *Wogs* and *Commies*. If *one* is used to make universal statements, then it is clear that in Freddy's eyes, blacks and Marxists have forfeited all claim to that universal *one*. And yet, beneath this arrogance is a guilty paranoia suggesting that he does in fact see the continuity between an anti-Semitic remark and the atrocities of Nazism. He feels that his unguarded remark has exposed him as a crypto-Nazi trying to avoid extradition to Israel—the novel is set at the time of the Eichmann trial. He even has a wild impulse to assure her, by way of a Germanically exhaustive catalogue (*Sturmbannführer, Obersturmbannführer, Superobersturmbannführer*) that he has not been involved in the Holocaust. The tone is obviously comic, but the connections are not entirely fanciful. As in many Spark novels, a nonutterance like this reveals the real anxieties Freddy's surface conversation is masking with diplomacy.

Freddy's failure to realize the meaning of national institutions other than his own is paralleled in his spiritual life, a life similarly limited—we are told that one pilgrimage along the Via Dolorosa has been enough for him. When, therefore, he brings his yardstick of absurdity to Barbara's dilemma, the opposing demands of church and private self, he is put out by her "immoderate" reaction:

> "Do you know," said this passionate spinster in a cold and terrifying voice, "a passage in the Book of the Apocalypse that applies to your point of view?"
>
> "I'm afraid the Apocalypse is beyond me," Freddy said. "I've never had the faintest clue what it's all about." . . .
>
> "It goes like this," she said, enunciating her words slowly, almost like a chant:
>
> *I know of thy doings, and find thee neither cold nor hot; cold or hot,*
> *I would thou wert one or the other. Being what thou art, lukewarm,*
> *neither cold nor hot, thou wilt make me vomit thee out of my mouth.*

Freddy did not reply. People should definitely not quote the Scriptures at one. It was quite absurd. (pp. 15–16)

This is a wholly Sparkian conversation, plaited out of two quite disparate strands and moving at cross purposes. (We have already encountered a similar scene in *The Girls of Slender Means*, that exchange between Nicholas and Felix Dobell.) Freddy privately ascribes strong feeling to Barbara, but no object; deep conviction, but no position. Feeling is something with which he generally tends to have little truck, and feeling isolated from an object is bound to seem even more "tiresome" because it has not been canalized to its proper end. And yet when that end *is* revealed to Freddy, he finds it absurd because it is "extreme." This standard response provides the cue for Barbara's sibylline outpouring about the church of Laodicea, and chitchat yields to prophecy. Freddy feels discomfited, and yet, although his shibboleth *absurd* and his use of the universal *one* are quickly invoked to restore his complacency, the encounter marks a turning point in his life.

Later in the novel we see him enter situations that would ordinarily have called for diplomatic detachment, as when he rebukes a woman in the shop of Alexandros for doubting the word of the proprietor (p. 55), and when he denounces his friends in Jordan for subscribing to beliefs and attitudes that were formerly his own. In a chapter called "A Delightful English Atmosphere," the element in which, up to this point in time, Freddy has moved and had his being, he uses the same text from Revelation that Barbara had applied to himself, though its grand seventeenth-century cadences are jumbled with contemporary ones.

But what of Barbara herself, the catalyst of this remarkable transition from detachment to passion? The chapter headed "Barbara Vaughan's Identity" begins with the very words that Freddy had inwardly used to respond to her rebuke, words that forbid people to quote the Bible at each other. That repeated sentence tends to hinge one aspect of her being, the English aspect, onto Freddy's own, but the resemblance stops there. Barbara's coming to Israel, while it is partly prompted by her affair with an archaeologist, is also to some extent a quest for unity of self. Our first prolonged exposure to her thoughts occurs on Mount Tabor, traditionally the site of the Transfiguration, of the colloquy between Christ and two patriarchs of the Old Testament. This interchange between representatives of the old and new dispensations helps plot the coordinates of Barbara's own position as a woman, half-Jewish, who has converted to Catholicism. Her impatience with her Israeli guides is our first indication of the contrary claims of materialism and spirituality—they bombard her with sociological and industrial information about Israel; she is interested only in the spiritual goals of pilgrimage. We know by now, however, that the opposition is not a straightforward one. Any responsible conception of the spirit must honor the matter in which it has its being. And since the divorce cannot be made glibly, it entails careful sorting and consideration, for very often the same facts are involved, and only the perspective differs:

> The tiring aspect of every journey she had made throughout the past three weeks was the hard work involved in separating the facts relevant to her point of view from those relevant to theirs. . . . By constitution of mind she was inclined to think of "a Catholic point of view" to which not all facts were relevant, just as, in her thesis-writing days, she had selected the points of a poem which were related only to the thesis. This did not mean that she failed to grasp the Christian religion with a total sense of its universal application . . . . All it meant was that her habits of mind were inadequate to cope with the whole of her experience, and thus Barbara Vaughan was in a state of conflict . . . . For she was gifted with an honest, analytical intelligence, a sense of fidelity in the observing of observable things, and, at the same time, with the beautiful and dangerous gift of faith which, by definition of the Scriptures, is the sum of things hoped for and the evidence of things unseen. (pp. 17–18)

Barbara's academic training has made it necessary for her to conceive of Catholicism as something apart from catholicity and the potential chaos of syncretism. She accordingly seems to suffer, at this stage of the novel at least, from what T. S. Eliot would call a dissociated sensibility. But as pattern banishes chaos, so chaos always threatens pattern. Any principle of order must eliminate or exclude the elements it cannot absorb, and faith is precisely such a principle. One of many intractable details threatening its capacity to pattern and make meaningful is Barbara's relationship with her fiancé. Later, during the sermon at the Altar of the Crucifixion, she will learn that the tidiness she is seeking is actually a chimera and that faith is not an archaeological quest, not a restoring of physical form to broken evidence. Faith indeed would be irrelevant if life were not as untidy and bewildering as Barbara finds it. Spark keeps that resolution in abeyance for the time being, however, and expects us to enter into her character's irresolute and unhappy state of mind. Its irresoluteness stems from a tension between her sense of *fidelitas* (her scrupulous, empirical method for acquiring and ordering knowledge) and *fides*, "dangerous" in the way it challenges the rational assumptions of that method with its untestable, unfathomable leaps. In Jordan, Barbara will learn to give up control of her destiny: passivity will pacify. At this stage of the novel, though, the elements of her heritage seem incoherent, and she is searching for the key that will help them coalesce.

Such a process must center on a principle of selection, and, while she cannot disregard the facts that the guides administer like inoculatory shots (as if to prevent infection by religious awe), those that are inessential need to be subordinated to those made significant by faith. The guides' miscellany of contemporary and scriptural information is shapeless, untouched by any quest for larger meaning:

> "I've really only come on a pilgrimage. I really only want to see the ancient sites. I'm really not interested in Scotch-tape factories."
> "We approach Beersheba."
> Suddenly, as it seemed, from behind a few palm trees Beersheba had appeared in a white dazzle of modern blocks reaching down to the great desert waves of the Negev. The desert lapped like a sea on the glittering strips of concrete that defined Beersheba's outlying blocks of flats.
> Barbara Vaughan said, "I'm really only interested in the Beersheba of Genesis." . . .
> "This is Beersheba, the birthplace of Jacob, the Father of the Twelve Tribes of Israel. We have a new school for immigrants. To teach them trades and Hebrew. I show you." (pp. 18–19)

The bathetic rhythm that oscillates pilgrimage with Scotch-tape factories and patriarchal history with trade schools is present in the description of Beersheba itself. It is made to seem chimerical by virtue of its *sudden* appearance, which also conveys the aggressive way in which it imposes itself on the landscape. At the same time, its formless and strident modernity is threatened with engulfment, as the statue of Ozymandias by desert sands. Just as trade schools jostle the spiritual meaning of the town aside, so the eternity of the landscape—which is the link with that meaningful past—is poised to expunge it. The Beersheba of Genesis, which is Barbara's object of pilgrimage, no longer exists as the Beersheba of Genesis. It is accessible only in an imagination activated by faith.

Unlike her guide, however, Barbara is blest with a double vision of the land, one that acknowledges the coexistence of the physical and the immaterial without allowing them to displace each other. While her sense of dualities might for the moment confuse her, it is also a source of enrichment. J. H. Dorenkamp has indicated in another context that the "person who has been granted such a vision no longer sees the world from only a temporal point of view, but rather *sub specie aeternitatis*."[3] For the moment, though, Barbara is confusing the archaeological with the anagogical and will necessarily suffer disappointment.

On p. 20 she is described as looking down on the green and blue of Galilee, while her mind, at the same time it absorbs the topographical details, also scans her personal life from the past through the present into the future. The problematical nature of her thoughts is enhanced rather than simplified by the all-embracing range of her vision and by its ability to synthesize rather than to exclude. This is apparent also in the "catechism" she receives from one of the guides, who sets his monoscopic view against her wider point of vantage. He accuses her of having betrayed her Jewish heritage by converting to Catholicism, which of course misconceives the *gift* of faith as a conscious dishonesty:

> Barbara had felt displaced, she felt her personal identity beginning to escape like smoke from among her bones. . . . "Who am I?" She felt she had known who she was till this moment: She said, "I am who I am." . . . Barbara had already begun to reflect that "I am who I am" was a bit large seeing it was the answer that Moses got from the burning bush on Mount Sinai . . . . The Catechism . . . stated that man was made in God's image chiefly as to the soul. She decided, therefore, essentially "I am who I am" was indeed the final definition for her. But the thesis-exponent in Barbara would not leave it at that. . . . The guide persisted in his point: Why had she turned Catholic? If she wanted a religion she was already a Jewess through her mother. Barbara knew then that the essential thing about her remained unspoken, uncategorized and unlocated. (pp. 23–24)

What is striking about this passage is its reliance on metaphors of space: "Barbara felt displaced"; "uncategorized and unlocated." The quest for identity in Israel, far from yielding answers, seems to have issued in even greater mystery, since the solution is to be found less in any tangible setting than in the realm of the spirit. Even at an intersection of eternal spacelessness and the human experience of space—Yahweh's meeting Moses—the ineffable is not explained, but remains grandly and inscrutably circular—"I am who I am." When Barbara uses this utterance in her own efforts at self-clarification, it will necessarily fail at the level of logic to yield any meaning—that which cannot be expressed in words is finally

3. "Moral Vision," 5.

inexpressible. The terms *Gentile* and *Jew*, which are the materialist terms that her guide is offering her, cannot begin to sketch the complexities and elusiveness of the soul itself. Thus, although her quoting Yahweh Himself seems at first to be sheer arrogance, it becomes apt enough when she recalls that the human essence, insofar as it images the divine, also finally defies verbal definition. The smoke that symbolizes her intangible selfhood connects with the smoke of the burning bush, while her inability to give satisfactory answers to the guide's interrogation depends on her having the "beautiful and dangerous *gift* of faith." Since what is given is not chosen, grace cannot be resolved into questions of human worth and volition. At the same time it is far from being the source of easy comfort. It is "dangerous" for two paradoxical reasons: in the first place it breeds the danger of complacency, the damnable "security" mentioned in *Macbeth*; and in the second, it threatens disequilibrium by issuing exorbitant demands and setting them against the less rigorous values of the world. Any solution for Barbara's dilemma that neglected to take account of her faith would automatically fail on the grounds of incompleteness, even if it offered the easy option simply of ignoring the source of her discomfort.

Atheistic humanism rejects belief in a Deity on the assumption that it somehow impairs the dignity and sufficiency of the person who entertains the belief. Such a person is seen to be guilty of surrendering existential heroism—a being alone in the universe—for illusory comfort. This charge cannot, however, be brought against the faith of Barbara Vaughan for the simple reason that the faith itself is *not* a source of solace. On the contrary, it requires difficult and anguish-ridden decisions and even puts her in physical danger, a point to which I shall return in the conclusion of this study. She has come to the Holy Land in search of her identity, and her identity will be seen later to inhere in her embracing, not in her explaining and rationalizing, the disparate elements of her heritage. This is a position of faith, one which Spark distinguishes from the humanistic vision of Freddy. When he suggests that Barbara disregard the church, his solution limits the terms of her dilemma instead of accepting them in all their problematic fullness. Small wonder that Barbara should reject this option with the vehement language of Revelation.

References to guides and travel abound throughout the novel, and it is through "irrational" journeys that the self is liberated into being, as in the interlude that allows Freddy to escape from the order and constraint of his diplomatic life. When he returns from the jaunt in Jordan, he recites Browning's "Through the Metidja to Abd-El-Kadr," significantly a *hodoporikon* (or journey poem) in which the object of the speaker's quest remains elusive:

> But he did not seem much concerned on this point, . . . and Hamilton recited, keeping time with his right hand:
>
> > *Could I loose what Fate has tied,*
> > *Ere I pried, she should hide*
> > *(As I ride, as I ride)*
> > *All that's meant me—satisfied*
> > *When the Prophet and the Bride*
> > *Stops the veins I'd have subside*
> > *As I ride, as I ride!*
>
> "I don't know in my head what it means," Abdul said, "but it means something in the blood-veins." (p. 92)

Abdul's reaction is the just one—it is by releasing the suppressed life of the unconscious, not by trammeling it in intellectual definition, that the poem (and the journeys of the novel) come to be invested with meaning. But even now Freddy is being reclaimed by his former self, and he reduces the value of the lyric to its virtuosity with rhyme. Indeed his obsession with rhyme divorced from meaning (he has written to an Oxford acquaintance on the same day, informing him that he has discovered a rhyme for *Capricorn*), like his parodies of medieval verse forms, points again to his concern with physical surface. In this he resembles Barbara's Israeli guide.

Barbara herself takes tentative steps toward resolving her crisis of identity in the solitude of Mount Tabor, which in addition to being a place of transfiguration is also a point of repose after the futile journeys and the hectoring guides:

> Barbara, on the summit of Mount Tabor, conscious of the Holy Land stretching to its boundaries on every side, reflected wearily upon her reflections. She thought, my mind is impatient to escape from its constitution and reach its point somewhere else. But that is eternity at the point of transfiguration. In the meantime, what is to be borne is to be praised. In the meantime, memory circulates like the bloodstream. May mine circulate well, may it bring dead facts to life, may it bring health to whatever is to be borne. (p. 27)

In Spark's novels, self-reflexiveness in a character often signals that he or she is on the verge of anagnorisis, something we have seen in the case both of Ronald and Nicholas. So when we find Barbara reflecting on her own reflections, we ready ourselves for a revelation that will cut to the heart of the book. Those reflections are not simply mental; they have an additional meaning of "images"—images thrown back at Barbara from the different racial mirrors of her childhood, the Gentile and the Jewish. An identity based on physical coordinates alone—like those supplied by the relentless interrogation of the guide—is likely to issue in limitation, just as the Holy Land, place of the Incarnation, is delimited by the boundaries she sees in the distance. And as the place is much less important than the anagogic events that happened there, so is Barbara's background less important than her spirituality. Any fulfillment of the self can occur only *sub specie aeternitatis,* and in the death that is God's prerogative to grant. In many Spark novels, as V. M. K. Kelleher notes, there is a "Hopkins-like conflict between time and eternity, between the vital, ephemeral processes of nature and the unchanging sphere of God."[4] Barbara, attacked here by a lassitude similar to that which haunts Ronald, is half in love with easeful death and the resolution it offers. Her dispiritedness and sense of life as something to be borne recall Daphne du Toit's cry in "The Go-Away Bird" just before her murder: "God help me. Life is unbearable."[5] Yet "bearing" can also have a natal sense, and what is to be borne encompasses what is to be born, the new potentiality of self that the subsequent adventures in Jordan will bring to light. The noble stoicism of the first kind of bearing (not dissimilar to Jean Taylor's in *Memento Mori*) is a necessary condition for the second, and, if sense cannot be imposed on life by the operation of the intellect, the circulation of the bloodstream, like the pulse in Browning's poem ("With a full heart for my guide, / So its tide rocks my side"), will offer meaning at a subliminal level.

Barbara's memory now yields up images from her separate childhoods in Bell Sands and Golders Green, images rendered with a rapt, Wordsworthian stationariness that detaches them from time and brings them to the threshold of eternity. The pain of resurrection is also hinted perhaps in the Eliotic hyacinths, sensed but unseen, and a strong sense of continuity ("So it must have been") offsets the momentous day when the son of a Tory family broke with tradition and decided to marry Barbara's mother. Their having "nothing left to say" also picks up the refrain of "The Curse of Cromwell," where Yeats similarly deplores the end of an aristocratic tradition. Just as the Israeli guide has accused her of betraying her Jewish heritage, so her father's family regard him as having

4. "Religious Artistry," 81.
5. Spark, *Collected Stories I,* 353.

betrayed his Gentile birthright. Both, it goes without saying, are unfounded charges, for both are based on racist premises:

> The air was elusively threaded with the evidence of unseen hyacinths. So it must have been before she was born, when the family understood that her father was going to marry the Jewess, and there was nothing left to say. . . .
> "Well, there's time for another set before you change and pack, Barbara," said Uncle Eddy, gazing out at the sky as if he could tell the time by it. The lawn lay beautiful as eternity. (pp. 28–29)

The lawn here resembles the Rye at the end of *The Ballad of Peckham Rye,* which is also transfigured in a "spot of time": "the Rye for an instant looking like a cloud of green and gold, the people seeming to ride upon it, as you might say there was another world than this."[6]

Barbara is about to leave this time-suspended milieu for Passover celebrations with her Jewish relatives, celebrations that also abolish consecutive time to affirm a symbolic continuity of the present with the past:

> "This is the poor bread which our fathers ate in the land of Egypt."
> Barbara had understood from her fifth year that it was not actually the same, wafery substance, here on the table at Golders Green, that had been baked by the Israelites on the first Passover night, and yet, in a mysterious sense, it was: "This is the bread which our fathers ate . . . ." (pp. 29–30)

The *inclusio* frames and eternizes the sacrament, and time is banished as much from Golders Green as from Bell Sands. Such parallels make it clear that the elements of Barbara's upbringing cannot be sorted into alternative categories, but must rather be seen to form a dichotomous unit, as balanced as the typological structures erected by the Fathers to harmonize Old Testament with New.

Harry Clegg, Barbara's lover, has the grace to see her whole (and she does him), whereas her English relatives, once again like the Israeli guide, perceive her taxonomically:

> The form of their love seemed to her to derive from a faculty of inner knowledge which they both possessed, a passionate mutual insight so unique in her experience that she felt it to be unique in human experience.
> Harry Clegg—shock-haired, unhandsome—who would have guessed he would be her type? Miles referred to him as "the red-brick

6. Spark, *The Ballad of Peckham Rye,* 202.

genius." But that was to reckon without Harry Clegg, who loved her. He loved her disguise as an English spinster not merely as disguise, but as part of her inexplicable identity. She was not an English spinster merely, but also a half-Jew, and was drawn to the equivalent quality in him that quite escaped both the unspoken definition "Englishman of lower-class origin," and the spoken one "red-brick genius." (p. 38)

Their affinity is based on a belief that the essential self is inexplicable and will simply be distorted by attempts to confine it in prejudicial molds, and their relationship combines both feeling and intellect, something the phrase "passionate mutual insight" suggests. Both of them elude the categories into which intellect or passion, operating separately from each other, might otherwise slot them, and so together they image a creative union that shuns stereotypes and celebrates uniqueness.

Such a fusion of spirit and matter, irradiated with a sense of purpose, has been seen in the earlier novels to be a "note" of religion, and Barbara's discomposure can be traced to the fact that her love for Harry has been blocked by the faith that till now has been her fund of meaning:

> Meanwhile she had been reconciled to the Church, in a frigid sort of way, as one might acknowledge, unsmiling, the victor in battle, in whose presence one is signing a peace treaty. She was obliged to repent. What of—the love affair? No, adultery, to be precise. Yes, but to be precise, it was impossible to distinguish the formal expression of her love from the emotion. "Go and repent," said the priest, worn-out with this involved honesty. "It was a love-affair," Barbara explained. "Yes, well, don't pretend it was the Beatific Vision." Barbara went so far as to repent that she could not repent of the forbidden love-making, and as is the plain expectation of all Christians she got the benefit of the doubt on the understanding that she put an end to the sex part of it. (p. 44)

The church has insisted on detaching the expression of the love from the love itself, since it cannot be sanctified without marriage. This is part of the painful sorting enjoined on Barbara, and not unnaturally she rebels. Her academic, questioning response to the dogma that more docile Catholics would simply take on trust can be measured by the weariness of the priest who finds that she cannot be fobbed off with formulas. At the same time, it is clear that Barbara has been muddling two distinct categories of love. We need perhaps to recall here that in Dante's beatific vision, separations in the universe are reconciled in the esemplastic unity of *caritas*:

O grace, unenvying of thy boon! that gavest
Boldness to fix so earnestly my ken
On the everlasting splendour, that I look'd,
While sight was unconsumed; and, in that depth,
Saw in one volume clasp'd of love, whate'er
The universe unfolds; all properties
Of substance and of accident, beheld
Compounded, yet one individual light
The whole. And of such bond methinks I saw
The universal form.[7]

It was Joanna Childe's mistake to confuse the primal and permanent character of *caritas* with mortal love, and to some extent it is
Barbara's too, since her confessor has to remind her that the two
orders of experience, while they might appear to have features in
common with each other, are not in fact the same. His separation of
the carnal from the divine seems from her present point of view to
involve a destructive fission, whereas her love for Harry has been
characterized by organic unity. There lies the rub.

Barbara's thoughts on Mount Tabor set out the dilemma in a
mock-psalmic format, which is also the sort of list that students of
history might draw up to systematize their understanding of an
event. The divine and the prosaic, as so often in Spark, come together and are superimposed. As though uttering a priestly versicle,
she asks herself why she does not cross the border into Jordan to
visit Harry, and then, like a congregation, offers her responses,
cause by cause. The chant of causes is interrupted midway by another statement of the versicle—the voice of worldly common sense
urging her to justify a delay that it cannot understand. The reason
adduced after this interruption—that it would be dangerous for
someone of Jewish blood to enter Jordan—differs from the others in
belonging to the realm of matter rather than of the spirit.

While Barbara agonizes over a conflict between two poles of
meaning in her life and struggles resolutely toward some sort of
reconciliation, Abdul Ramdez has created an identity in precisely
opposite terms. His is a chameleonic adaptability that cocks a snook
at allegiance of any kind, whether it be spiritual or physical. This is
the structural function—one of qualifying contrast—served by the
strange scene in Acre that, in the chronology of the novel, coincides
with Barbara's excursion into Jordan. The narrator takes us into
Barbara's mind and lets us inspect the turmoil there, confident that

---

7. *The Vision, or Hell, Purgatory, and Paradise of Dante Alighieri*, 480–81.

the coordinates of her dilemma, because they are fixed, will eventually declare themselves. She has no such confidence in the presentment of Abdul, however. Because he has chosen to create a self-protecting mystery about his true motives, Spark seems to feel that she had better furnish the facts intrusively and authoritatively for fear that the reader will be misled by his smoke screens. Abdul represents a generation of young people that, wearied by the demands of ideology, has sloughed them off. The author's treatment is sympathetic to the extent that it finds some meaning in their abrogation of meaning, but I disagree with D. J. Enright's claim that "it almost looks as if, in this context of raging religions, obsessive politics and racial confrontations, the author's sympathies are with the non-committed, with 'the young or the young in heart who belonged to nothing but themselves.'"[8] The novel is predicated on ideas of commitment and would deconstruct itself if this were the case. Selfhood defined as "belonging to nothing but itself" is a notion that Spark has always taken care to expose. She reveals its presence behind the solipsism of Seton, for example, and would no doubt trace it ultimately to the *non serviam* of Satan. Her position is much more that of Pascal as versified by Keble ("Spite of yourselves, ye witness this, / Who blindly self or sense adore; / Else wherefore leaving your own bliss / Still restless seek ye more?"). So when a character like Abdul decides that the easiest way of dealing with the situation is to behave with impenetrable foolishness, we are left in no doubt that this is at best a provisional solution, and one that would hardly answer to Barbara's dilemma. Avoiding the exhaustion of commitment, he has chosen a career of immaturity, shutting himself into the frame of childhood. Vocation to a life of perpetual enchantment, while it might have charm, is also feckless, even if detachment from a cause makes possible that sense of ridicule which Spark endorses in "The Desegregation of Art."

Her treatment of Abdul and his fellows is thus ambivalent. While their touch seems refreshingly light after the vehement nationalism of the Israeli guide, they are still spineless hedonists—latter-day lotus-eaters. (As Conrad has noted, the abomination fascinates, and we see the effect of this fascination when, in her subsequent fiction, Spark concentrates more and more on Abdul's equivalents among the cosmopolitan wealthy—an emphasis that leads to the impoverishment of the novels in question.) Abdul and his Israeli friend have bridged their cultural barrier not by the strenuous effort of syn-

8. "Public Doctrine and Private Judging," 563.

thesis that Barbara is bent on making, but by dissolving the cultures themselves into a soup of anarchy. As in the VE celebrations described in *The Girls of Slender Means*, Spark uses the passive to suggest the mental surrender of the drug addicts, for whom kef and marijuana have replaced ideology. Their howls and convulsive dances, like the uninhibited emotionalism of Hubert's cult in *The Takeover*, are also proof of faulty self-control. Whereas Barbara has been seen exalted on a mountaintop, a traditional place of theophany, Abdul chooses the chemical exaltation of drugs in his effort to forge a meaning for his life, and whereas she attempts to effect a fusion of resistant elements, he and Mendel simply throw them together. Their meaning is in fact the nonmeaning of Absurdism, where sacred chants become the vehicle for juvenile onomatopoeia, and the cadences of the psalms are adapted to accounts of Nazi atrocities against the Jews and of Jewish atrocities against the Arabs. Here is a foretaste of the Abbess of Crewe, who chants secular lyrics to the plainsong of her offices. It is obviously a solution of sorts, but it is the unstable solution of mixture, not the chemistry of compound. And it can be applied only on the periphery of the societies it attempts to bridge, and only at an unreal witching hour. Still, it is by entering the world of Abdul and Suzi Ramdez that Freddy for a while breaks out of his carapace of prejudice, and Barbara similarly moves to a clarifying and integrative decision. The feast of misrule was, after all, designed to exorcise unruly elements of the psyche by giving them free rein. In the words of Peter Kemp, Freddy and Barbara "both experience regeneration through a kind of emotional late-flowering."[9] This is to some extent made possible by their readmission to the rowdy and disaffected world of adolescence.

The next phase of the novel presents the gradual recovery of Freddy's memory, miming his process of slow recollection in its fragmentary design. We are taken back to a point in time after his escapade in Jordan, a time when Freddy is trying to regain a sense of normality. His denunciation of the Cartwrights (in terms similar to Barbara's of him) now seems unaccountable (p. 133), and the energy and passion that measured their lukewarmness has dissipated. Even so, there are Delphic touches to his post-Jordan conversation, and he keeps telling the puzzled Cartwrights that he has premonitions of bloodshed. But the bloodshed of his prophetic visions has nothing to do with Barbara, as at first he fears, and everything to do with his mother's death at the hands of a servant she has been

9. *Muriel Spark*, 118.

bullying for years. Thus does another routine—a domestic one—suffer the irruption of apocalyptic violence. The detachment of Freddy's former life has been modified, and he deals with the "nightmare" of involvement by projecting it into a calmer future, as Aeneas does in a storm. "It'll make a jolly good story one day" (p. 134) adds up to a contemporary paraphrase of "forsan et haec olim meminisse iuvabit" (*Aeneid* 1.203).

Freddy, unlike Barbara, has not had a problematic past to sort through and order. His life, in its endless diplomatic sameness, has simply been a self-replicating pattern. The mindlessness of habit is indeed implicit in the last image he recalls before the onset of amnesia. He remembers having seen Joanna Cartwright struggle with a food parcel like countless Englishwomen of his experience whose habits of "charity" have been unaffected by the foundation of the welfare state, and also having seen her husband barge past her without offering any help—an equally typical sight (p. 136). His amnesia from this point is described in terms of records mislaid, a fit metaphor for the nature of Freddy's life hitherto, a life of bureaucratic routine. Its shapelessness and want of resolution can be gauged from the way his letters to his mother are desperate recyclings of stock items and from the way in which his function as problem-solver is divorced from any sense of solution. We are told that his mother does not want answers to her problems so much as an excuse to involve Freddy in her life. Even before he dashes off to Jordan with Barbara, he sees her demand that he come home as a demand for human sacrifice and resists it, obscurely aware that the routine would stifle the faint individuality remaining to him. It is clear also that he perceives routine to be entirely distinct from the regulation and discipline of a religious vocation. This is exemplified by the monk of the Potter's Field, who has always fascinated Freddy. A Sparkian note is struck by the hen-coop this votary tends in the midst of what appears to be a continuous religious transport. The hens signify the intractability of matter, acknowledged, not discarded, by the aspirations of the soul:

> The all-over properties and associations of this spot were hallowed by a small, musty Greek Orthodox shrine and that ancient, frail monk who was sublimely unaware of anything in the world around him except his hen-coop and God; within the latter category were included all of the human race who crossed his territory on their sightseeing tours or smuggling business, for he seemed to look right through them into God, and treated all accordingly with mesmerized awe, having very few words actually to say to them. Freddy had always found this

old monk extremely satisfying company. One could talk to him without effort of conversation; the monk would express all that was necessary in the pose of his shrivelled body under its loose blue robe, and in
the light of his dark eyes, enormous in their deep bony sockets. (p. 141)

Christian spirituality has a tradition, represented by such figures as
George Herbert, John Keble, and Jean-Pierre de Caussade, of finding God not in momentous mystical flights but in "the trivial round,
the common task." Freddy's is a routine unsanctified by purpose, in
contrast with the monk's, which has found the unworldly in the
world, the transcendent in the mundane. The religious carries with
him an absolution from small talk, that strenuous and tiresome
need upon which Freddy's professional and private life (they are
virtually synonymous) have been erected, and to which the domestic babble of his letters home bears witness.

It comes as no surprise, therefore, that when Freddy breaks forth
from his shell, it is to the monk that his thoughts turn. He provides
an image of spiritual disencumberment, seeming only accidentally
to be entrammelled in his blue cassock:

> Freddy, in this first hour of his absence, turned and looked up towards
> the field; he could see from where he stood on the footpath a project-
> ing angle of the monk's quarters, and caught a glimpse of the blue
> cassock as it seemed to potter about the yard, bearing the old man's
> spiritual bones and constitution inside it. He is rounding up his hens
> for the night, thought Freddy, and at that moment the thought also
> went through his head that, if necessary, he could spend the night up
> there. . . .
>   It did not occur to Freddy that there was something irrational in
> this notion. (pp. 141–42)

Later that same evening he has an epiphany of purpose, though its
object is left mysteriously vague. The detail of this "spot of time," on
the other hand, projects an integration of natural and urban land-
scapes, a commingling of the hills that Psalm 121 associates with
divine help and the city whose epithet "Old" necessarily brings to
mind the transfigured, Apocalyptic "New." Behind the detailed topo-
graphic coordinates there seems to lurk the pre-Copernican assumption that Jerusalem is the center of the universe, an assumption
which gives further point to the search for meaning that Freddy is
poised to undertake:

> The sunset was at its climax, touching the spires and hills of Jerusalem
> so that they seemed to rise from vague darkness; in the east the Mount
> of Olives with its three summits, the Hill of Offence, the Hill of Olivet,

and the Hill known as the Viri Galilaei; to the west, Mount Gareb; and in the north, the Scopus range. Freddy went down as if to meet them, for in the illusory light the mountains had seemed to mingle with the domes and minarets of Old Jerusalem. He suddenly knew what he was looking for, he knew his first task . . . . (p. 143)

Throughout the narrative of the escapade, Spark keeps recurring to Freddy's later, bewildered efforts at reconstructing it, and on one occasion uses one of her favorite images—the cloud of unknowing:

> Saturday night to Tuesday afternoon: the events were to come back to Freddy in the course of time; first, like an electric shock of fatal voltage, but not fatal, and so, after that, like a cloud of unknowing, heavy with molecules of accumulated impressions and finally when he had come to consider the whole mosaic of evidence, when he had gathered the many-coloured fragments of what actually happened, and had put the missing parts in place, then he came to discern, too late for action but more and more clearly as the years sifted past, that he had been neither a monster nor a fool, but had behaved rather well, and at least with style and courage. Looking back at the experience in later years Freddy was amazed. It had seemed to transfigure his life, without any disastrous change in the appearance of things; pleasantly and essentially he came to feel it had made a free man of him where before he had been the subdued, obedient servant of a mere disorderly sensation, that of impersonal guilt. And whether this feeling of Freddy's subsequent years was justified or not, it did him good to harbour it. (pp. 147–48)

The cloud of unknowing is of course the metaphor applied by a medieval mystic to the ineffable experience of God, and the fatal shock that is not fatal in Spark's adaptation of the symbol is the death of self and the heightening of spiritual faculties that attends upon it. The details of the experience are in fact inessential, for a buried allusion to Shelley's *Adonais*—"Life, like a dome of many-coloured glass, / Stains the white radiance of Eternity"—shows that its core lies beyond the "many-coloured fragments of what actually happened." Enslavement to a sort of existential guilt (its impersonality distinguishes it from the religious kind) has prompted those endless letters to his mother that he flushes down a lavatory during his "freedom," and also his endless society verses apologizing for a want of dinner-table brilliance. What has seemed to impose order has in effect been the cause of spiritual dystrophy. When this vanishes, alertness and receptivity come in its stead, as witness the way in which he absorbs the beauty of Alexandros's house, where an oriental carpet discloses its loveliness in a slow epiphany. Also of note is the way in which he puts in abeyance that sense of racial difference that usually affects his dealing with people who are not English. We are told that he regards the house of Alexandros as though it were the house of a westerner with an interest in oriental artifacts, an attitude which, while it might at first seem unrepentantly Eurocentric, marks a clear advance on the Freddy revealed to us at the start of the novel.

The section is framed by a projection of his transfigured reality, matching the earlier vision in which city and landscape merged. Here the prayers of the muezzins fill each sector of the heaven with prayer, overarching the religious divisions that the physical directives evoke (Israel; convent; Holy Sepulchre). The eagle is presented in medieval bestiaries as a bird that renews its life in the sun, and it is moreover the emblem of St. John, popularly supposed to be the writer of Revelation:

> Freddy waited. The night now began to give out the chanting of the minarets, from Israel across the border to the west of the convent, then nearer, to the north, from the direction of the Holy Sepulchre. It was three o'clock. The chanting voices echoed each other from height to height like the mating cries of sublime eagles. This waiting for the return of Alexandros was one of the things Freddy was to remember most vividly later on, when he did at last remember the nights and days of his fugue. From the east, beyond the Wailing Wall, a white-clad figure raised his arms in the moonlight and now began his call to prayer, and soon, from the south, then in the south-east, and from everywhere, the cry was raised. (p. 155)

Fugues comprise a polyphony of braided voices, not dissimilar to the voices of the muezzins in the sky above, and while they derive their name from the Latin word for flight, they are supreme exemplars of musical purpose and control. Freddy's "fugue" is both these things, human volition expressed in escape and a divine summons to a fuller life all wound together in a pattern. Like St. John of Patmos, Freddy has heard "a great voice of much people in heaven, saying, Alleluia; Salvation, and glory, and honor, and power, unto the Lord our God" (Revelation 19:1).

While Freddy's flight is a flight from nullifying routine, Barbara's flight takes the form of escaping from the convent that has given her bed and board. It is rendered in romance terms that recall the finale of *The Eve of St. Agnes:*

> She glanced behind and upward, and could not place her sense of something unaccomplished in the silence. The front door was

unlocked and Freddy now held it open so that the moonlight flooded her last footsteps from the sleeping convent. They had got away. . . .

And what would she have said if one of the nuns had caught them, if one of them came to the door even now that she was getting into the car, lifting the Liberty dressing-gown as if it were a long evening dress and she departing from a late night party? "My dear good woman, things are not what they seem, as you in the religious life ought to know. Foolish virgin, hasn't experience taught you to expect the unexpected?" (pp. 159–60)

Much Spark criticism acknowledges that the author, like Sandy Stranger in *The Prime of Miss Jean Brodie,* is concerned with transfiguring the commonplace—Nancy Potter is one of many commentators to point out that the "process of transfiguration of the apparently unspectacular into a parable of good is a noticeable aspect of the novels."[10] The departure from the nunnery, treated as though it were a chivalric episode, needs an element of combat to keep it true to form. It is its absence that Barbara feels as a "sense of something unaccomplished" when she leaves, and she supplies the lack in one of those conversations that never take place (like Nicholas's with Felix). The motif of transfiguration here is derived from the Cinderella fable (a dressing gown becomes a ball dress or even, via a pun on the type of fabric, the vestment of Liberty personified). Barbara offers the nun a discourse on the Second Coming, based on the parable of the wise and foolish virgins. This urges vigilance for the *parousia*, for the imminence of transfiguration, though here it is Freddy who has come like a thief in the night and has liberated her from that semblance of infertility and constraint that the world has imposed upon her. So it is that the convent becomes a symbol of the old self, divested of its contradictions and divisions for a new, harmonized vision, a vision centered in paradox rather than contradiction. As Jay Halio has noted, the "escape from the convent symbolizes . . . Barbara's shedding of certain nun-like attitudes once and for all":[11]

For the first time since her arrival in the Middle East she felt all of a piece; Gentile and Jewess, Vaughan and Aaronson; she had caught some of Freddy's madness, having recognized by his manner in the car, as they careered across Jerusalem, that he had regained some lost or forgotten element in his nature and was now, at last, for some reason, flowering in the full irrational norm of the stock she also

10. "Muriel Spark: Transformer of the Commonplace," 115.
11. "Muriel Spark: The Novelist's Sense of Wonder," 273.

derived from . . . . She had caught a bit of Freddy's madness and for
the first time in this Holy Land, felt all of a piece, a Gentile Jewess, a
private-judging Catholic, a shy adventuress.

. . . It was not any escape from any real convent, it was an uniden-
tified confinement of the soul she had escaped from; she knew it
already and was able to indulge in her slight feeling of disappointment
that they had not been caught. (pp. 173–74)

As so often in Spark, the *inclusio* of the first of the two paragraphs
above is designed to seal off a crucial discovery in the frame of an
epigram, and the deleted conjunction in the phrase "Gentile Jewess," coming as it does after "Gentile and Jewess," gives the integration an even greater indivisibility.

Part of what Barbara is escaping is a life of nonsacramental
celibacy with her friend Miss Rickward, who embodies the routine
from which, in a different form, Freddy is also fleeing. Her vision is
cyclopic, as incapable of paradox as it is of humor. Spark reveals
her prosiness in a letter on p. 164 that is full of litotes and clumsy
negative formulations. It must be set against the almost mystic rapture of Barbara's vision after the flight from the convent. Here
Spark paraphrases the famous epistemology of the spirit set forth in
Tintern Abbey when she tells us that the starlight of the sky that
Barbara is gazing at is half-perceived, half-created as if by contact
with her exalted state of mind. In this there is a true approach to the
beatific vision she had imagined her love for Harry to embody.

The section of the novel that follows this revelation is one of the
most intricately structured in a book of structural intricacies. Inter-
leaving the immediate past with the present of Barbara's reverie,
Spark presents the intrusion of everyday fact upon the adventure as
of history upon timelessness. What is crucial here is the fact that the
individual's will has been surrendered (p. 181) and peace found in
passivity: "E'n la sua volontade è nostra pace." There have, however, been earlier intimations of the wholeness offered by the escape
from the convent. This can be gathered from the way in which she
has begun to view Jerusalem. The exclusive polarities on which her
identity has until now foundered have yielded to a rich typological
tension, one which merges duality and simultaneousness, past,
present, and anagogical future, all in a single act of attention:

. . . Barbara had concentrated her driving in the area round Jerusalem . . . and enjoyed gazing over to Bethlehem or to the Mount of
Olives, and, on a clear day, the domes and walls and rooftops of Old
Jerusalem. She would stop the car at various points, day after day, as
she discovered the best angles for sighting her target.

> Jerusalem, my happy home,
> When shall I come to thee?

The lines sped to mind, and simultaneously seeing in her mind's eye the medieval text to which she was accustomed and, with her outward eye, an actual Gethsemane passively laid out on the Mount of Olives across the border, she sensed their figurative meaning piled upon the literal—"O my sweete home, Hierusalem"—and yearned for that magnetic field, Jerusalem, Old and New in one.

> When shall I look into thy face,
> Thy joys when shall I see? (pp. 180–81)

This layers the spiritual upon the literal, the New Jerusalem, envisaged in the poem as a place exempt from suffering, upon the Old. Thus the literal, while not losing its reality, is subordinated by an indefinite article to a wider, soterial view—"an actual Gethsemane" functions as metonymy for the idea of salvation. This is precisely the thrust of the sermon on Calvary that Barbara hears once she has crossed the border between the realm of matter and spirit, as well as that between Israel and Jordan:

> If you are looking for physical exactitude in Jerusalem it is a good quest, but it belongs to archaeology, not faith. . . . The historical evidence of our faith is scattered about under the ground; nothing is neat. And what would be the point of our professing faith if it were? There's no need for faith if everything is plain to the eye. We cannot know anything perfectly, because we ourselves are not perfect. When we have come to perfection in time, then faith, like time, will be done away. "We have an everlasting city," St. Paul has said, "but not here; our goal is the city that is one day to be." (pp. 213–14)

The antitype of the sermon in the book's design is the Eichmann trial, which Barbara attends shortly before her crossing. While the priest at the Altar of the Crucifixion cautions against fetishizing facts at the expense of the spiritual growth they are meant to engender, Eichmann represents a materialism that has deified routine and severed it from any sense of the abomination it was designed to serve. His is a pervertedly "religious" submission of the will to a perverted plan—another vocation parodied and inverted, and constituting what William McBrien has called "the ultimate divided self."[12] Eichmann's reactions are those of an automaton, incapable of empathy. If they were, the massacre would naturally never have occurred. But if Eichmann is a computer, incapable of paradox,

---

12. "Muriel Spark: The Novelist as Dandy," 168.

Barbara is his very opposite. Her vision is so constituted as to make the perception of duality possible. Eichmann, inured to the claims of the spirit, can relay only his robotlike directives from Bureau IV-B-4. Small wonder, therefore, that the narrator should invoke the spiritless factuality of the *nouveau roman* and the self-reflexive *nausée* of Beckett's *Waiting for Godot* to render the quality of the trial. In its negative way, this too has provided an epiphany about the nature of self and how it cannot allow itself to be extinguished by the claims of institutions. Intelligent acquiescence rather than mechanical assent—that is the Dantesque hallmark of beatitude—and the serenity of Barbara's newfound purpose enable her to integrate Judaic practices with her Catholicism: "she had touched the Wailing Wall for Saul Ephraim and prayed, but unobtrusively . . ." (p. 195).

One feels, once the sermon has run its course at the Altar of the Crucifixion, that the main business of the novel has been transacted. What follows tends to move down a gear into the complications of plot that we find in thrillers and farces. Spark has complained to Ian Gillham that the book fails to "race" in the manner of her other novels,[13] but this strikes me as being less than entirely true. The last pages, written with the impatience of a "racer," certainly do gallop along. But it is not the tempo that is at fault so much as their tendency to go out of thematic focus. When, for example, Miss Rickward approaches Barbara for directions, assuming her to be an Arab maidservant, the tension is almost entirely the tension of plot—is her disguise about to be penetrated?—and the relief is relief at the resourcefulness of farce, as when, say, Figaro is able to explain an apparently inexplicable situation to the Count Almaviva. There is no enriching symbolism in the deflected encounter—it remains a literal, though exciting, incident. And the improbable twists and tergiversations that make up the rest of the novel also seem very little removed from the giddy unreality of farce, so much so that when Barbara tells Freddy that Miss Rickward is pursuing her, he assumes that her fever has caused her to rave (p. 222).

Even the aphorisms yielded by the escapade in Jericho seem, like some of Nicholas Farringdon's observations, too flat to warrant the chiastic closure that Spark usually applies to her moments of epigram: "'I was thinking that life is love.' 'Very profound. And love is life.'" Still, there might be some thematic or structural point to the protracted running-down of the novel, a De Quincian knocking at the Mandelbaum Gate. The epiphany has occurred and must some-

13. Gillham, "Keeping It Short," 412.

how be preserved through all the flurry of a plot in need of resolution. As Joseph Hynes rightly observes, "Barbara's intensely authentic moment of integration renders her more than ever aware of the difficulty of making it last."[14]

Little meditations in the midst of all the frantic coming and going show that Barbara does manage to incorporate that moment, and that the selective nature of her vision has learned a new habit of catholicity. Her belief in the omnipresence and omnipotence of God makes her a tranquil eye in the stormy action:

> From being confined with the fever like this, Barbara Vaughan had taken one of her religious turns and was truly given to the love of God, and all things were possible. And she thought, we must all think in these vague terms: with God, all things are possible; because the only possibilities we ever seem able to envisage in a precise manner are disastrous events; and we fear both vaguely and specifically, and I have myself too long laid plans against eventualities. . . . It would be interesting, for a change, to prepare and be ready for possibilities of, I don't know what, since all things are possible with God, and nothing is inevitable. (pp. 285–86)

A further illustration of this spiritual repose can be found in her observations to Suzi as they complete their circuit of the Christian shrines:

> "Well, either religious faith penetrates everything in life or it doesn't. There are some experiences that seem to make nonsense of all separations of sacred from profane—they seem childish. Either the whole of life is unified under God or everything falls apart. . . ." She was thinking of the Eichmann trial, and was aware that there were other events too, which had rolled away the stone that revealed an empty hole in the earth, that led to the bottomless pit. So that people drew back quickly and looked elsewhere for reality, and found it, and made decisions, in the way that she had decided to get married, anyway. (pp. 307–8)

The metaphor of the stone inevitably suggests the empty tomb of the Resurrection, that archaeological vestige of an event that cannot be limited in space or time. At the same time, it converts to the *profundus lacus* of the Requiem's offertory prayer, the eternal vacancy of hell. (Hell is defined in modern Catholic theology as the absence of God.) Any attempt at drawing a line between the God-filled and the Godless, or between the evidence for faith and faith itself, must therefore issue in meaninglessness.

14. *Art of the Real*, 55.

This is perhaps the point of the novel's coda, where Freddy walks through Old Jerusalem, enumerating all the gates and the various events of salvation that they memorialize (the triumphal entry into Jerusalem, the martyrdom of St. Stephen). He does so without any feeling for their spiritual significance and thus reduces them to guidebook features, on a level with the purely accidental way in which the gate of the title was named, the gate which Peter Davison has termed "the central image of the heroine's life—half Gentile, half Jew by birth, Catholic by faith and choice":[15]

> . . . Damascus Gate, that gate of the Lord's triumphal entry into Jerusalem on Palm Sunday, and Herod's Gate. He walked around the city until . . . he came to the Mandelbaum Gate, hardly a gate at all, but a piece of street between Jerusalem and Jerusalem, flanked by two huts, and called by that name because a house at the other end once belonged to a Mr. Mandelbaum. (p. 330)

15. "The Miracles of Muriel Spark," 140.

4

The Abbess of Crewe

Vocation Travestied

The novels we have bypassed in our leap from *The Mandelbaum Gate* to *The Abbess of Crewe* are works in which, because Spark wears her Catholicism rather more lightly, the theme of vocation, if it is foregrounded at all, is thoroughly secularized. La Rochefoucauld says that our virtues are frequently but vices disguised, so perhaps the frigid chic we find in the works of this period is the vice that, properly "disguised," had yielded the elegance and detachment, say, of *The Bachelors*. The epigrammatist is always a potentially heartless being, striving to compact and pattern the sprawl of human life to a state of tidiness so perfect that it borders on the inhumane. As long as Spark's Catholicism is there in the background to warm and humanize the chillness that any striving for perfection entails, all is well. When her religious convictions are effaced or overshadowed, though, her fiction becomes merely clever. The features of middle-period Spark are internationalism of the most glib and superficial kind, a detachment so thoroughgoing that it amounts to heartlessness, and an austerity of detail, a "minimalism," that makes the novels seem denuded and skeletal. Robert Hosmer has said of a recent Spark novel, a throwback to the spare mode of the seventies, that its author is "always economical and efficient, so efficient that, before the first chapter of *The Only Problem* concludes, we know all the main characters and the plot as well."[1] It would seem from this that the line between efficiency and attenuation is very easily crossed.

The Abbess of Crewe is a masterly jeu d'esprit, and its light touch discourages us from taking it too seriously. But in many respects, not least its thin "efficiency" and its elegant heartlessness, it is of a

---

1. "The Book of Job: The Novel of Harvey," 442.

piece with the other novels of the middle period. Although it resumes the themes of dedication and selfhood, their treatment has been infected by the typical stances of this phase, and it gives us surreal perversions of the religious life, akin to those of secular life in *The Hothouse by the East River*. But whereas the last treats events from purgatorial nonhistory, the doings of the abbess claim a different relation to reality—they aspire to the artifice of myth, shutting out the debasement (and, at the same time, the sanity) of the world at large. Her vocation proves in the long run to be that of Yeats in "Sailing to Byzantium," which is to say an insentient, amoral "permanence," achieved at the cost of life itself. As William McBrien has noted, she espouses an "irreligious, because inhuman, transcendence."[2]

Although God is the final cause of religious vocation, He scarcely features in the narrative of *The Abbess of Crewe*, His presence displaced by the woman whose electronic surveillance parodies His omnipresence and omniscience. The vacuum created by this godlessness, however, is not the chill, life-denying vacuum of *The Driver's Seat* and *Not to Disturb*, but rather the saturnalian vacuum of the feast of fools, which also had its being out of time. Enid Welsford has suggested that these festivities possibly derived from "an ancient intercalary period inserted into the calendar to fill the gap between the solar and lunar years. Such a period might well be regarded as lying outside the usual course of events and therefore a fitting season for turning the world upside down."[3]

A decidedly blasphemous atmosphere prevailed in some French towns during this extratemporal riot, for, to quote Welsford yet again:

> As soon as the higher clergy shed their authority the ecclesiastical ritual lost its sanctity. Even the Mass was burlesqued. Censing was done with pudding and sausages. Sometimes an ass was introduced into church. . . .
>
> On these occasions solemn mass was punctuated with brays and howls, and the rubrics of the "office" direct that the celebrant instead of saying *Ite missa est*, shall bray three times. (p. 200)

Horseplay of this bacchanalian order is not the abbess's style, but she does substitute claims of blood for claims of grace and secular verse for divine office. The envoi of the novel, quoting Prospero's

2. "Muriel Spark: The Novelist as Dandy," 173.
3. *The Fool: His Social and Literary History*, 199. Henceforth cited parenthetically in the text by page number.

"Our revels now are ended," and the persisted use of the present tense, as though the book were a set of stage instructions (with dialogue), both contribute to the sense of its being a pageant. It registers as an ephemeral masque, with as little relevance to the march of history as the abbey itself. Ostensibly a Catholic, the abbess is in fact an antinomian, sealing off her order from the directives of postconciliar Catholicism, which, for her, is hopelessly contaminated with time, and substituting her own fiats for those of God and His Church.

In the novels up to *The Mandelbaum Gate,* Spark seems generally to suspect people who act in defiance of the Church's claims, though we see Barbara flirting with the possibility in her decision—never put to the test—to marry her fiancé in the face of an ecclesiastical ban. However, in the light of the Second Vatican Council, which unleashed turmoil in a body otherwise known for its uncompromising solidity, such positions of obedience seem a shade futile. It is possible even to detect touches of authorial sympathy for the abbess in her defiance of the "new-look" Rome. This sympathy does not necessarily invalidate the workings of the satire, as John Updike thinks it does when he complains that putting "in the mouth of your villainess poems of your own cherishing—such paradoxes make indifferent satire but good art."[4] On the contrary, it strikes me that "indifferent satire" is the satire of simplifying dismissal, while the compound of contempt and attraction makes rather for complexity.

Spark's stance seems exactly that of Pope toward Belinda in *The Rape of the Lock,* a poem which has obviously provided the inspiration for the thimble theft upon which the action of the novel turns. It is an attitude formed from detachment, amusement, dismissal, and fondness. Much has been made of the allegorical connections between the events of the Watergate affair and those of the Abbey of Crewe, and the author herself has confirmed these in her interview with Sara Frankel: "I thought the Watergate episode was very interesting, it was completely exaggerated. The Americans created a big national thing of it, and I thought, well, if they lived in Europe and knew about corruption—all governments are corrupt—they would realize that it was like a nun's quarrel over a thimble."[5]

But the allegory at another level embraces such ecclesiastical malcontents as Archbishop Lefebvre, trenching on heresy himself because he senses heresy in the body that should denounce it. It

4. "Topnotch Witcheries," 78.
5. Frankel, "Interview," 444.

would seem that Spark's cynicism ("all governments are corrupt") includes the major factions within the Church, both of which receive short shrift. In the words of Velma Richmond, the "rivals are . . . caricatures of extreme Catholic views held after the Second Vatican Council. They are both examples of the excessive romanticism that Spark presents as dangerously destructive."[6]

Whereas the novels that precede it in the canon have presented their material in a crisp, transparent way, *The Abbess of Crewe* begins in puzzlement and cuts back to an explanatory prelude only at the start of Part 2. The procedure is obviously meant to intensify the surrealism[7] that gives the work its distinctive flavor—something apparent from the very start, where we find the abbess discussing surveillance with one of her nuns. This topic is in itself a startling one, and startling also is the artfulness of the superior, concealed by her artless endorsement of the "traditional" methods of spying. Irony inheres in the epithet *receptive,* for the abbess has bugged the avenue of poplars through which they are walking. Her mind (too rigid to admit of receptivity) has given the virtue over to the machines that have become her surrogate ears and eyes:

> "What is wrong, Sister Winifrede," says the Abbess, clear and loud to the receptive air, "with the traditional keyhole method?"
>
> Sister Winifrede says, in her whine of bewilderment, . . . the mind where no dawn breaks, "But, Lady Abbess, we discussed right from the start—"
>
> "Silence!" says the Abbess. "We observe silence, now, and meditate." She looks at the tall poplars of the avenue where they walk, as if the trees were listening. The poplars cast their shadows in the autumn afternoon's end, and the shadows lie in regular still file across the pathway like a congregation of prostrate nuns of the Old Order. The Abbess of Crewe, soaring in her slender height, a very Lombardy poplar herself, moving by Sister Winifrede's side, turns her pale eyes to the gravel walk where their four black shoes tread, tread and tread, two at a time, till they come to the end of this corridor of meditation lined by the secret police of poplars.[8]

The unease we associate with surrealism becomes apparent at once in the inversion of "clear and loud." Wrenching this idiomatic

6. *Muriel Spark,* 134.

7. Long before *The Abbess of Crewe* was written, Charles Alva Hoyt drew attention to surrealistic elements in the art of Muriel Spark in his "Muriel Spark: The Surrealist Jane Austen."

8. Spark, *The Abbess of Crewe,* 9–10. Henceforth cited parenthetically in the text by page number.

doublet, the author suggests an artificially alert enunciation, and compounds the oddity by moving from command ("Silence!") to sweetly uttered statement ("We observe silence now, and meditate"). The description of the trees is also unsettling. What seems at first to be a tired pathetic fallacy—"as if the trees are listening"— energetically turns to fact as soon as we realize that the avenue is fitted with microphones. And while the trees thus turn into receivers, the abbess herself, as in some Walt Disney cartoon, is transformed into a tree, tramping shadows-turned-nuns underfoot as she sweeps along. She treads the prostrate shadows of her fellow poplar-nuns as if by feudal right, for the "Old Order" translates "ancien régime" as much as it does the preconciliar Benedictine rule. This play with metaphor is entertaining in a mischievous way, but it also illustrates the abbess's knack of mimicry. She responds to her surroundings like a chameleon, able to be a tree to trees, a funnel to ships, and all things to all people. At the end of the paragraph, the trees have abandoned their tired Romantic postures of listening and have straightened up to become a surrealist phalanx of policemen. Nothing is stable in the novel, and this protean shiftiness in the description of the trees and of the nun who walks through the corridor they form is symptomatic of the way in which things will come into, and go out of, focus throughout the narrative.

The abbess's values are those of an unashamed county snob, untouched by the spirit of the Christianity she professes. It is her perspective as much as the author's that sets her elegance against the "undistinguished" appearance of Sister Winifrede and appropriates a virginal phrase from the *Litaniae Lauretanae* (*turris eburnea*) while Winifrede's earthly handsomeness is presented as a virtual sin of the flesh (or so the oxymoron "carnal chastity" would seem to imply):

> Strangely, she is as tall as the Abbess, but never will she be a steeple or a tower, but a British matron in spite of her coif and her vows, and that great carnal chastity which fills her passing days. . . .
>
> "In we go to Vespers whether you like it or whether you don't."
>
> "But I love the Office of Vespers. I love all the Hours of the Divine Office," Winifrede says in her blurting voice, indignant as any common Christian's, a singsong lament of total misunderstanding.
>
> The ladies walk, stately and tall, but the Abbess like a tower of ivory, Winifrede like a handsome hostess or businessman's wife and a fair week-end tennis player, given the chance. (pp. 10–11)

In Christian thought, outward profession is meant to answer to inward truth—a tenet that goes back at least as far as the prophet

Joel, who urges the people to rend their hearts and not their gar-
ments. But for Alexandra all that matters is the appearance of sanctity. Attending office is a duty; it is the equivalent of social "good
form" and must be observed whether the spirit be willing or not.
Indeed, it is *better* done when not. By protesting her love of the
office with such "vulgar" intensity and enthusiasm, Sister Winifrede
is missing the point as Alexandra conceives it and aligning herself
with the conventional believers whom the latter holds in social and
theological contempt. At a later stage of the novel she will even go
so far as to say that a bourgeoise proclaims her belief and believes in
the "wrong things," while a "lady" secretly believes in nothing. If
this were not so utterly zany, it would be horrifying, but we have to
recall that the story exists in the ontological vacuum of farce and of
the animated cartoon, where potentially evil actions seem funny
because the victims cannot suffer: they are blest with an inhuman
resilience and elasticity. In *The Abbess of Crewe* all conventional
attitudes and assumptions are turned on their heads. The point of
monastic dress, for example, is that it covers social difference and
affirms the rule of poverty, but the abbess makes judgments on style
and social bearing as though the religious life were simply an extension of her former social one. Similes such as the one derived from
tennis playing and the world of businessmen x-ray the covering
habit and make social allocations of the wearer that are quite foreign to the spirit of the rule.

Alexandra's own garment, moreover, is simply a version of haute
couture, flattering rather than neutralizing the beauty of the woman
who wears it, and who ensures its *physical* immaculateness by
changing it twice a day. "Changing habits" can also mean "changing
norms," however, and the phrase additionally refers to the abbess's
protean ability to adapt herself to her changing circumstances, to
survive by camouflage. Like her convent, she herself defies classifi-
cation, at one moment more radical than the most extreme postconciliar theologian, at another more conservative than the most ultra-
montane:

> The Abbess stands in her high place in the choir, white among the
> black. Twice a day she changes her habit. What a piece of work is her
> convent, how distant its newness from all the orthodoxies of the past,
> how far removed in its antiquities from those of the present! "It's the
> only way," she once said, this Alexandra, the noble Lady Abbess, "to
> find an answer always ready to hand for any adverse criticism what-
> soever." (p. 12)

The allusion here to Hamlet's "What a piece of work is man" gives to the abbess the blasphemous role of creatrix and usurper of deity. It is *her* convent, a pronoun properly belonging to the *Deus Artifex*. The point is reinforced later at the Office of Lauds, where she claims the nunnery as her own with another possessive pronoun, and an allusion to Genesis presents it as having been recreated in her own image. She looks down in wonder at her chapel as though it were fresh from creation and, like God Himself, she were seeing that it is good. Spark also notes that her thoughts center on the fullness of her being, a blasphemy that scarcely needs expounding when we recall that the "full existence" comes close to paraphrasing the doctrine of the pleroma. Yet a note of bathos is struck by the high chair on which she is sitting, and which could as well furnish a nursery as evoke the throne of God.

Alexandra, having recreated the abbey in the image of the world in order to save it from the world, exploiting the apparatus of modernity in order to keep modernity at bay, is ready to apply all expedient means—no matter how unspiritual—to secure the end she has in mind. So it is that she conceives the various religious orders within the Church as sorts of business enterprise, capable of the same mergers and ruthless self-advancement. The novel's ever-present surrealism surfaces in the conjunction of these dissimilars in the passage below. It is compounded by a strange reference to the Joachite "heresy" and misapplied advice from St. Paul to be all things to all people. Unconnected thoughts are often a sign of madness, and so too are zanily absolute statements with no evidence to support them. Why Alexandra should think that we have entered the age of the Holy Ghost is never made clear—Joachim, to do him justice, offered reasons for his unorthodox belief:

> "In these days," the Abbess had said . . . , "we must form new monastic combines. The ages of the Father and of the Son are past. We have entered the age of the Holy Ghost. The wind bloweth where it listeth and it listeth most certainly on the Abbey of Crewe. I am a Benedictine with the Benedictines, a Jesuit with the Jesuits. I was elected Abbess and I stay the Abbess and I move as the Spirit moves me." (p. 13)

The secret of effective surrealism is perhaps its deadpan nature: the oddest assemblage of detail is presented without visible discomposure. We see this especially in the abbess's sangfroid when a reporter crosses the chapel window outside, a silhouette against the blue and the yellow of the glass (p. 13). What sounds for all the world like a Chagall brought to life is shrugged off as a subject unworthy of notice or, at best, a listless hypothesis or two. Such invasions of the world into a closed community are among the lesser paradoxes of a novel playfully bent on amassing as many as it can to mystify and entertain its readers.

Nor is the entry of the world into the nunnery limited to the presence of policemen and reporters: spiritual intrusions match the physical. We soon learn that the abbess is declaiming a love poem in counterpoint to the Benedictine office. The other nuns, seeing that her lips are not synchronized with theirs, assume she is using the Tridentine text, but this conservative appearance actually masks a secularity far more extreme than any espoused by Sister Felicity, Alexandra's postconciliar rival. The abbess's "canticle" is in fact Marvell's "To His Coy Mistress":

> The Abbess moves her lips in song. In reality she is chanting English, not Latin; she is singing her own canticle, not the vespers for Sunday. She looks at the file of tombs and, thinking of who knows which occupant, past or to come, she softly chants:
>
> > *Thy beauty shall no more be found,*
> > *Nor, in thy marble vault, shall sound*
> > *My echoing song; then worms shall try*
> > *That long-preserved virginity . . . .*
>
> The cloud of nuns lift their white faces to record before the angels the final antiphon:
>
> > *But our God is in heaven:*
> > *he has done all that he wished.*
>
> "Amen," responds the Abbess, clear as light. (p. 15)

Another inversion of traditional Christian dogma can be found in this classic example of the *carpe florem* topos. *Carpe florem* addresses death in order to devote itself more sensuously to the world, whereas its ascetic equivalent, *memento mori*, contemplates death to prepare for eternity. Alexandra's double-exposure of pagan attitudes upon a divine text parallels other phases of secularity in the Church, as when, during the Renaissance, the pectoral cross of Pope Alexander VI contained an image of Aphrodite. Whereas the nuns as a whole are concerned with the *lux perpetua* of eternity, their abbess has centered her thoughts on the "nox . . . perpetua una dormienda" we find in Catullus's carpe diem lyric. The simile ("clear as light") that describes her assent to the psalm thus becomes acutely ironical.

For as long as the surrealism is contained within the limits of

Alexandra's vision, the novel remains faintly plausible. But there are occasions when it extends into the whole convent and produces effects of disconcerting zaniness, as in the refectory, where a nun moves serenely from the rule of St. Benedict to a manual of recording technology:

> Her voice is nasal, with a haughty twang of the hunting county stock from which she and her high-coloured complexion have at one time disengaged themselves. She stands stockily, remote from the words as she half-intones them. She is reading from the great and ancient Rule of St. Benedict, enumerating the instruments of good works:
>
>> *To fear the day of judgement.*
>> *To be in dread of hell.*
>> *To yearn for eternal life with all the longing*
>> *of our soul . . . .*
>
> Quietly, the reader closes the book on the lectern and opens another that is set by its side. She continues her incantations:
>
>> *A frequency is the number of times a periodic*
>> *phenomenon repeats itself in a unit of time.* (pp. 17–18)

Vocation is ordinarily conceived as the submission of the individual to the divine will. In the strange, inverted world of the abbey, the individual will subsumes the divine in a feast of misrule.

This engulfment of the one will by the other also produces megalomania, in which an individual fiat becomes the semblance of a cosmic one. Joseph Hynes is not the only one to entertain doubts about the "mental competence"[9] of the abbess who has tried to approximate beatitude by abolishing time, an abolition imaged by the present tense through which the novel moves:

> "It is absurd in modern times that the nuns should have to get up twice in the middle of the night to sing the Matins and the Lauds. But modern times come into a historical context, and as far as I'm concerned history doesn't work. Here, in the Abbey of Crewe, we have discarded history. We have entered the sphere, dear Sisters, of mythology. My nuns love it. Who doesn't yearn to be part of a myth at whatever price in comfort? The monastic system is in revolt throughout the rest of the world, thanks to historical development. Here, within the ambience of mythology, we have consummate satisfaction, we have peace." (p. 20)

It is almost impossible to disentangle the skeins of sympathy and mockery in the tone here. Spark has always invoked religion as a yardstick to judge the perverseness of the world, but now that post-

9. *Art of the Real,* 113.

conciliar Catholicism has lost some of its reassuring stability, the yardstick lacks the rigidity essential for measurement. Modernism, with its insistence on the relativity of doctrine, has begun once again to haunt the Church, and it is on modernism that the abbess, like Lefebvre, has visited her contempt. She is no doubt entitled to her conservative stance, but the logic behind it is peculiar to say the least. How can history be said "not to work," as if it were some sort of mechanical invention and not the irresistible deposit of time?

In rejecting modernism and the history that allows it to make its adaptations, Alexandra is therefore also to some extent rejecting reality, and in that rejection lies the possibility of madness. Madness is also akin to surrealism, whose reality is the free-associative reality of the dream, not of rationally explicable nature, and also, perhaps, a close neighbor of "mythology." The fantastic fusion of horse and man in the centaur or the projection of an aerial war maiden in the Valkyrie, for example, are surreal imaginings quite as bizarre as the creations of a Dali or a Breton or an Abbess Alexandra. But mythology, because it is ritual and infinitely repeatable, is also the locus of archetypal truth. So indeed is religion, even a religion that, like Christianity, marries infinity with time in the doctrine of the Incarnation. The abbess is thus an ambivalent figure, seen to be doing the wrong thing for the right reason, in reverse of T. S. Eliot's St. Thomas.

Alexandra elaborates her position further in conference with her henchwomen:

> "The more scandal there is from this point on the better. We are truly moving in a mythological context. We are the actors; the press and the public are the chorus. Every columnist has his own version of the same old story, as it were Aeschylus, Sophocles or Euripides, only of course, let me tell you, of a far inferior dramatic style. I read classics for a year at Lady Margaret Hall before switching to Eng. Lit. However that may be . . . the facts of the matter are with us no longer, but have returned to God who gave them. We can't be excommunicated without the facts. As for the legal aspect, no judge in the kingdom would admit the case, let Felicity tell it like it was as she may. You cannot bring a charge against Agamemnon or subpoena Clytemnestra, can you?" (pp. 24–25)

Again, good sense and insanity are indivisibly present in this discourse. In *The Public Image*, Spark shows how journalists, even though they are meant to traffic in facts, are often as guilty of fanciful constructs as Alexandra herself. But facts that have been lost to the sensationalism of the media are not the less factual for having vanished. What has happened has, intractably, happened. This, at any rate, would seem to be the point of the epitaph, paraphrased from Job, on facts that return to God their maker. In His consciousness, Berkeley style, their ontology is guaranteed. Myths by the same token are the slow accretions of time, not the manufactured fables of an individual like Alexandra, who, like her White House equivalent, has attempted to destroy the facts that call an official "scenario" into question. Indeed, they are even less manipulable than history, for their growth in the collective unconscious cannot be monitored, and thus distorted by unscrupulous journalistic intervention.

It is true that books like Carl Bernstein and Bob Woodward's *All the President's Men,* with their signal codes and gothic meetings in parking garages, can take on the vividness and suspense of novels, and it is true also that Felicity is vulgar enough to "tell it like it is," a cliché that the abbess holds in pincers to show her scorn of the charge. But while the abbess happens to be right in these particular instances, it is true also that only insane people draw a frame around reality and apply to it the aesthetic "laws" of discourse instead of moral ones. George Greene says of Alexandra that "she suffers from a fatal ignorance about the distinction between technique and truth,"[10] a distinction Walburga uses to puncture the abbess's rhetoric about bringing a charge against Agamemnon and placing Clytemnestra under a subpoena: "You can . . . if you are an actor in the drama yourself" (p. 25).

Alexandra's confusions of life and art are not innocent and spontaneous, however, but rather designed to make any reconstruction of the real events impossible. This is a fair way of describing the art of the novel itself, formed from precisely such a tangle—"The more truths and confusions the better" (p. 26). Spark herself has said, "I don't claim that my novels are truth—I claim that they are fiction— out of which a kind of truth emerges. And I keep in my mind specifically that what I am writing is fiction because I am interested in truth—absolute truth—and I don't pretend that what I'm writing is more than an imaginative extension of the truth—something inventive."[11] No scrupulous observation of this boundary can be found in Alexandra's fictions, on the other hand. At the same time that she aspires to godhead, she aspires to authorship, and, as Sue Kimball

10. "*Du Côté de Chez Disaster*: The Novels of Muriel Spark," 309.
11. Frank Kermode, "The House of Fiction: Interviews with Seven English Novelists," 80.

has pointed out, the abbey becomes a "microcosm of the world, which the novelist-figure, the Abbess, tries to rearrange."[12]

As *The Abbess of Crewe* unfolds, so the abbess's plot is unscrambled, and the author slowly discloses the ratio between "absolute" truth and Alexandrian fiction. She starts her disclosures on p. 13. Her mock-epic interrogative—"How did it start off without so much as a hint of that old cause, sexual impropriety, but merely from the little misplacement, or at most the theft, of Sister Felicity's silver thimble? How will it all end?"—parodies the invocation to the muse in *The Rape of the Lock*:

> Say what strange Motive, Goddess! cou'd compel
> A well-bred *Lord* t'assault a gentle *Belle*?
> Oh say what stranger Cause, yet unexplor'd,
> Cou'd make a gentle *Belle* reject a *Lord*?

The imbroglio that follows is as fantastic as anything in Pope's satire or in its informing model, Boileau's *Le Lutrin*; and yet some shrewd observations about Church practice *do* lodge in its coils. When Alexandra turns to Sister Gertrude for advice on how to deal with the convent's notoriety, commentators have been swift to note the resemblance her advisor bears to Henry Kissinger. But at the same time his endless diplomatic juggling with payoffs and losses is being pilloried, so too is the dogmatic relativity of modernism:

> "She's in a very wild area just now, reconciling the witch doctors' rituals with a specially adapted rite of the Mass," Mildred says, "and moving the old missionaries out of that zone into another zone where they are sure to be opposed, probably massacred. However, this will be an appropriate reason for reinstating the orthodox Mass in the first zone, thus modifying the witch doctors' bone-throwing practices. At least, that's how I see it." (p. 29)

This rickety chain of dependences occurs in such nursery rhymes as "The House That Jack Built" and is also the pattern of the mad logic that Alexandra applies to the abbey itself. But while the abbess might for a brief moment enjoy the endorsement of the narrator when she pours scorn on Gertrude's activities, that endorsement is withdrawn the moment she herself veers off on a lunatic trail of her own:

> "I don't know why she goes rushing around, spending her time on ecumenical ephemera. It has all been done before. The Arians, the

12. "Intentional Garble: Irony in the Communication of Muriel Spark," 91.

Albigensians, the Jansenists of Port Royal, the English recusants, the Covenanters. So many schisms, annihilations and reconciliations. Finally the lion lies down with the lamb and Gertrude sees that they remain lying down. Meantime Sister Gertrude, believe me, is a philosopher at heart. There is a touch of Hegel, her compatriot, there. Philosophers, when they cease philosophising and take up action, are dangerous." (pp. 28–29)

One of Alexandra's favorite couplets is that from *The Garden* ("Annihilating all that's made / To a green thought in a green shade") which celebrates a return to paradisal timelessness. Her annihilation is of a different order, however—the annihilation of facts that get in her way. Her disregard for real distinctions is as radical as that shown by Sister Gertrude when she attempts to synthesize Christianity and witchcraft by leaping several barriers. Alexandra is quite right to dismiss her "ecumenical" busyness (not far removed from such real ecclesiastical excesses as Communion with bubblegum and mineral water), but any sympathy she might gain from this is at once called into question by the cavalier list of heresies invoked to support her dismissal. This lumps together the English recusants (persecuted for their loyalty to Catholicism during the reign of Elizabeth I), the Covenanters (fanatical Presbyterians opposed to the liturgy of the Church of England), and traditionally heretical heretics such as the Albigensians. It is not doctrinal impurity that concerns Alexandra so much as the fact of rebellion, rebellion which riles her aristocratic sense of order. So at the very moment her criticism seems just (as when she inveighs against Gertrude's imperious forcing of the messianic hour, "Finally the lion lies down with the lamb and Gertrude sees that they remain lying down"), its justness is overturned by the flanking insanity. We are left with a queasy instability that is the essence of surrealism—indeed, Barbara Keyser goes so far as to suggest that Spark has "limited her depth of field so that sickness, death, the ugly scramble for worldly power stand out in sharp clarity while life, health, and beauty remain hazy and unfocussed."[13]

Although Alexandra has doubts about Gertrude's nugatory obsession with the time and the world that she herself has decreed out of existence, she needs still to consult her:

"Gertrude," says the Abbess, "Sister Gertrude has charmed all the kingdom with her dangerous exploits, while the Abbess of Crewe continues to perform her part in the drama of *The Abbess of Crewe*.

13. "Muriel Spark's Gargoyles," 38.

The world is having fun and waiting for the catharsis. Is this my destiny?"

"It's your calling," says Gertrude, philosophically.

"Gertrude, my excellent nun, my learned Hun, we have a problem and we don't know what to do with it."

"A problem you solve," says Gertrude.

"Gertrude," wheedles the Abbess, "we're in trouble with Rome. The Congregation of Religious has started to probe. They have written delicately to enquire how we reconcile our adherence to the Ancient Rule, which as you know they find suspect, with the laboratory and the courses we are giving the nuns in modern electronics, which, as you know, they find suspect."

"That isn't a problem," says Gertrude. "It's a paradox."

"Have you time for a very short seminar, Gertrude, on how one treats of a paradox?"

"A paradox you live with," says Gertrude, and hangs up. (pp. 30–31)

Having made the world over as a Greek tragedy, Alexandra has supplanted Christian free will with inflexible *ananke* and converted vocation into destiny. Two quite separate notions of calling and ordaining blur into each other to form a paradox. Paradox is essentially static, being incapable of resolution, as Gertrude points out, and therefore fit only for contemplation out of time. But Alexandra's dilemma centers on the fact that although time no longer applies to the abbey, she has forged her paradoxical rule from age and modernity, elements of time, and thus stands accountable to a world in which time is driving to the linear resolution she cannot face. Thus it is that the novel has neither catharsis nor peripeteia and that it ends with a journey toward rather than an arrival at. But Gertrude, inhabiting the temporal world beyond the abbey walls, is also reduced to an endless sorites of theological trade-offs. The stasis of resolution that both of them seek exists only in paradise.

Whereas the exchange between the nuns is playful and arch, with a Learian internal rhyme in one of the vocatives ("Gertrude, my excellent nun, my learned Hun"), the letter that Alexandra sends to Rome replays its content in stately slow motion and turns conversation into brocaded Renaissance prose. It reads in fact like a formal *contentio*, solemnly swinging between opposing points of view. Relaying Gertrude's advice in this way, and with Occam's razor glinting brightly in her hand, the abbess dismantles the problem by defining it out of existence. Logical and epistemic truth are obviously not the same thing, but she takes care to equate them and

gets herself out of a tight corner by arguing logically from out-
rageous premises:

> Your Eminence does me the honour to address me, and I humbly
> thank Your Eminence. . . .
> I have the honour to reply to Your Eminence. I will humbly divide
> Your Eminence's question into two parts. That we practise the
> activities described by Your Eminence I agree; that they present a
> problem I deny, and I will take the liberty to explain my distinction,
> and I hold:
> That Religion is founded on principles of Paradox.
> That Paradox is to be accepted and presents no Problem. (p. 32)

This is Barbara's solution in *The Mandelbaum Gate*, and obviously
to be respected as a bringer of peace, but when it is applied to an
abbess's megalomaniac designs it is distorted out of recognition, for
surrealism takes what is unquestionable and secure and gives it a
horrifying unfamiliarity. We have only to recall how Dali makes
watches spill over the side of a table, and how Buñuel suggests that
a cloud's passing over the moon is somehow commensurate with a
blade that slices open an eyeball.

The novel now cuts back to a point before the crisis, cinemat-
ically established by that ill-fated thimble:

> In the summer before the autumn, as God is in his heaven, Sister
> Felicity's thimble is lying in its place in her sewing-box.
> The Abbess Hildegarde is newly dead, and laid under her slab in
> the chapel.
> The Abbey of Crewe is left without a head, but the election of the
> new Abbess is to take place in twenty-three days' time. After Matins,
> at twenty minutes past midnight, the nuns go to their cells to sleep
> briefly and deeply until their awakening for Lauds at three.
> But Felicity jumps from her window on to the haycart pulled up
> below and runs to meet her Jesuit. (p. 37)

The section begins by repeating the Vespers antiphon—"But our
God is in heaven"—meant in its cheery way to pick up Browning's
lyric from *Pippa Passes*, and so to give to Sister Felicity's thimble
the serenity of a snail on a thorn. By means of some mischievous
anaphora, Spark relates the repose of the thimble to the repose of
the late abbess. Breaking with this timeless world of peace and
predictability, with its office recited at set hours and its nuns sleeping in their cells, is the disruptive Sister Felicity, ever the indi-
vidualist as she dashes off to a tryst with her Jesuit lover. Popular
novels and biographies have often shown nuns "jumping over the

wall" à la Monica Baldwin. The surrealist mode of Spark's novel takes what one imagines to be the topoi of these convent novelettes and subverts them. The pastoral cliché of the romp in the hay seems to be travestied in the haywain into which Felicity jumps, her veil no doubt streaming on the wind. Another cliché, the climactic run of lover to lover so favored by Hollywood, likewise turns to farce as soon as one imagines the habit churning away above Felicity's tiny legs and the equally billowy advance of the Jesuit in the opposite direction. Felicity's rivals are quick to point out that Jesus has been displaced by Jesuit in her vocation to the religious life:

> "What are we here for?" says Alexandra. "What are we doing here?"
> "It's our destiny," Mildred says.
> "You will be elected Abbess, Alexandra," says Walburga.
> "And Felicity?"
> "Her destiny is the Jesuit," says Mildred. (p. 38)

These three plotters are not very far removed from their prototypes in *Macbeth*, though Walburga somehow manages to hold back an "All hail" before prophesying "You will be elected Abbess." Having dealt summarily with the vocation of the McGovernesque rival, they now say spiteful things about her workbox, blasphemously equating it with a text from Revelation. The dialogue's elegant frigidity derives from the comedy of manners, but surrealism is responsible for the bizarre modulations into realpolitik:

> "Felicity's sewing-box is the precise measure of her love and her freedom," says Alexandra, so soon to be Abbess of Crewe. "Her sewing box is her alpha and her omega, not to mention her tiny epsilon, her iota and her omicron. . . . How strong is her following?" . . . Walburga says sharply, "This morning the polls put her at forty-two percent according to my intelligence reports." (p. 39)

Spark even has the abbess approach the satanic declaration *non serviam*: "Keep watch on the popularity chart. Sisters, I am consumed by the Divine Discontent. We are made a little lower than the angels. This weighs upon me, because I am a true believer" (p. 43).

Caught between these demonic factions, the nuns themselves provide a silent and long-suffering electorate, to be manipulated in a power struggle one would not ordinarily imagine to be part of the religious life. And yet the authorial voice, tinged as it is with Alexandra's own, is not charitably disposed toward them. Their actions are rendered as a mechanical unison, and the synecdoche that registers those actions has the effect not of giving them a more vivid presence, but rather of reducing them to Miltonic "blind mouths":

The forks move to the faces and the mouths open to receive the food. . . . A less edifying crowd of human life it would be difficult to find; either they have become so or they always were so; at any rate, they are in fact a very poor lot, all the more so since they do not think so for a moment. Up pop the forks, open go the mouths, in slide the nettles and the potato mash. They raise to their frightful little lips the steaming beakers of water and they sip as if fancying they are partaking of the warm sap of human experience, ripe for Felicity's liberation. (p. 61)

The tone of uncharitable contempt in this description nudges Spark's satire toward the Juvenalian mode and recalls Ronald's attacks of *nausée* in *The Bachelors*. Indeed we are startled to find the snobbish intonation of the abbess in phrases such as "frightful little lips" and, looking in vain for her presence to explain it as free indirect speech, have to admit that it is the author who is speaking in this unpleasant way. There is no effort at the kindly redress that Ronald attempts when he arraigns his friends during one of his brainstorms. Spark has retracted the reassurance of a norm, for neither the protagonists nor the faceless chorus they manipulate carry her endorsement. It is worth recalling that Ronald's vocation had the effect of individuating the man, of taking up his human peculiarities into his religious life and sanctifying them there. Vocation in *The Abbess of Crewe*, by contrast, has the effect of nullifying the individual soul or, in the case of Alexandra, sinfully aggrandizing it with aspirations to godhead.

A calling to the religious life ought to center on *contemptus mundi*, but here that profession of contempt is inverted. The contemners are despised in turn: ". . . the ordinary nuns, grown despicable by profession, file into the sewing-room and take their places" (p. 72). "Profession" has the dual implication of "vows professed" and "occupation," so that self-abasement is seen to have become a job as ordinary as the practice of medicine or law. Indeed, it is only when sin begins to color and delineate the mass that the collective identity begins to dissolve and the nuns are said to show, "in their discontent, a trace of individualism at long last" (p. 73). Generally, though, the background nuns are subordinated to the greater realities of appetite, whether it be for food or for power.

These two appetites converge when Alexandra courts her Jesuits, and the courtship centers on an enticingly prepared tea tray. (One is reminded of the coffee-drinking episode in *The Rape of the Lock*, where appetite is similarly ritualized.) The nun who brings in the tray is a spectral presence, much less vivid than the food she is carrying (p. 64). Later still, it is carried away by a nun who is reduced to a dark form, while the tray continues radiantly and unequivocally to be a tea tray (p. 67). The connection between identity and ingestion is also touched on when Alexandra consults Gertrude, her oracle on the green line:

> "The salvation of souls comes first," says Gertrude's husky voice. "The cannibals are to be converted to the faith with dietary concessions and the excessive zeal of the vegetarian heretics suppressed."
> "What puzzles me so much, Gertrude, my love, is how the cannibals will fare on the Day of Judgement," Alexandra says cozily.
> "Remember, Gertrude, that friendly little verse of our childhood:
>
> > *It's a very odd thing —*
> > *As odd as can be —*
> > *That whatever Miss T. eats*
> > *Turns into Miss T . . . .* (pp. 51–52)

The spiritual cannibalism of the nunnery has precisely the same effect—of assimilating the mass of individuals to the power-seekers, who devour the identity of the nuns to secure their allegiance. When Alexandra tells Sister Winifrede she could gobble her up were it not that she loathes suet pudding, she sounds like an ogress in a fairy tale. Food also generates other comic moments in the novel. At first sight the abbey menus seem designed to mortify the flesh like the penances of the ascetic saints, but we soon realize that the austerities—nettles, water, tinned cat food—are subsidizing Alexandra's appetite for paté and wine.

One can almost forgive Sister Felicity her bad temper when she gets wind of these injustices, but she is otherwise presented as an ineffectual antagonist, fugitive or absent as she misses Office or scurries after her Jesuit. It is true that she forms a weak negative charge to Alexandra's positive quest for power, but Spark withholds her endorsement and leaves us reeling about in the satiric vacuum, trying in vain to get our moral bearings in a world where every person is held up to scorn. Joseph Hynes formulates our dilemma as a choice between "an intelligent and hypocritical snobbish totalitarian on the one hand and a small-minded and equally hypocritical espouser of a drab-looking new day on the other hand."[14] It is an impossible choice to make. Felicity's reforms are too obviously expedient, too blatantly interested to carry much weight, and Spark hints her own impatience with her ideology when she

14. *Art of the Real,* 112.

associates it with tepid water. At the same time, we cannot assent to the snobbery of Hildegarde and Alexandra (and even, implicitly, the snobbery of the author) when they call her "a common little thing." They speak slightingly about her and about her workbox behind her back. Alexandra is even malicious enough to say spiteful things about her in her presence. Hildegarde resembles her successor in her nastiness and in her tendency to take religious forms and put them to uses so bizarre that they trench on blasphemy. Hence she refers to the workbox and to Felicity herself as trials of the flesh to be embraced in a spirit of self-mortification (pp. 47 and 71–72). A sort of apostolic succession thus exists between the abbesses, since both subscribe to the same distorted values and both share delusions of omnipotence. The "here" of Hildegarde's discourse on the beauty that she and Alexandra have chosen to hide from the sight of humankind is ostensibly the "here" of the convent, but also at the same time the "here" of the sublunary world, of which she and her successor claim to have God-like knowledge. Their deific awareness of their loveliness, as in the epistemology of Bishop Berkeley, is enough to give it substance. Equally blasphemous is their belief that their beauty passes human understanding. The infinitely recessed self-mirroring of each in the vanity of the other presents itself as a parody of the begetting of the Son by the Father, for this, as it is phrased in *A Portrait of the Artist as a Young Man,* derives from the Father's contemplating "as in a mirror His Divine Perfections . . . thereby begetting eternally the Eternal Son."[15] Throughout the book, Spark uncharitably stresses Felicity's plainness and her tiny stature, offset by Alexandra's magisterial height. Her face is described as being tiny and bad-tempered when she discovers that someone has been meddling with her workbox on p. 72, while two pages later, her "little" body is shown to be convulsed with rage.

    Because Alexandra has an angelic beauty and Felicity a dwarfish ugliness, Alexandra is quick to conceive her as a Satan figure, rebelling against divine service (as the abbess herself rebels against the Church). Spark extends this mock demonology in her recurring allusions to the Compline preface (from the Epistle of St. Peter): "Brethren, be sober, be vigilant; because your adversary the devil, as a roaring lion, walketh about, seeking whom he may devour; whom resist steadfast in the faith." The majesty of the satanic lion is travestied in the miniature petulance of Felicity's moods, which are also rebuked by Alexandra in a paraphrase of St. Peter on p. 77.

---

15. James Joyce, *A Portrait of the Artist as a Young Man,* 152.

We have already seen how Alexandra herself is haunted by the same "satanic" wish, one even more imperious in scope. Like Felicity, she refuses to serve. Vocation in the abbey is conventional to the extent that it involves the submission of judgment to faith—but one does not have to read very far to realize that this is a faith in personalities, not in God. When Alexandra threatens to expel Winifrede if she fails to obey her, she does so in terms that call the latter's vocation into question and as though she had the omniscience to judge (pp. 80–81). Thus does she usurp the place of God and reenact the first sin in heaven. The command "be sober, be vigilant" and its variants come back again and again like voices in a fugal stretta, not least when Alexandra delivers the devilish electoral speech that secures her victory (pp. 84ff.). In this address, which attacks the reformist spirit of Felicity, she equates ecumenism with the democratic leveling of class. Old Catholicism, by this token, becomes equated with "family," reform with vulgarity. Her homily ends with an account of aristocratic and bourgeois behavior that seesaws surrealistically *ad feminam* between Felicity and herself. She notes, for example, that only a bourgeoise would keep her love letters in a workbox or copulate in a poplar avenue. The whole list betrays an obsession with form at the expense of spirit—as witness the counseled secrecy of disbelief so long as the practice of faith be maintained. On the other hand, Felicity can justly be charged with the exaltation of spirit above form, an imbalance of which Spark is equally scornful.

Indeed nobody in the novel manages a satisfactory balance. An author who affirms that "all governments are corrupt" is presumably reluctant to validate any one party at the expense of the other. Felicity is dismissed as a petty petite bourgeoise, but how can one endorse a dismissal based on snobbish precepts, and instate in place of the demoted woman an abbess who behaves like a witch to celebrate her victory?

> Whereupon they join hands, the three black-draped nuns, Walburga, Alexandra and Mildred. They dance in a ring; light-footed; they skip one way then turn the other way.
> Walburga then says, "Listen!" She turns her ear to the window. "Someone's whistled," she says. (p. 91)

We are back in the world of *Macbeth*, even if it is *Macbeth* reconceived by a Disney animator. The calls of succubus and incubus in Act 1, Scene 1 may have been replaced by the whistle of a Jesuit, but the glee of the three nuns is true to their Shakespearean prototypes—

glee at having equated of fair and foul, and so created what will later be termed a "garble."

The "garbled" status of Alexandra's speech is proved, among other things, by her claim to be nobly descended from St. Margaret Mary Alacoque, in fact the daughter of a notary. Facts are beside the point, though, once one has entered the realm of mythology. We see the three sisters blatantly rewriting history (in the manner of the journalists in *The Public Image*) so as to salvage their reputations against Felicity's charges:

> "In fact," says the Abbess, "they do have a romp."
> "And the students take away the thimble—"
> "Could it be a sexual symbol?" ventures Mildred. (p. 95)

Their fiction need have only the internal consistency of myth. So, when in one of her allotropic metaphors (poplar, lightning conductor, and funnel are others), the abbess becomes an obelisk—emblem of a dubious text—the irony is especially marked (p. 100). Facts scrambled with truth give rise to garble, and it is in garble that myth can be realized:

> "Garble is what we need, now, Sisters. We are leaving the sphere of history and are about to enter that of mythology. Mythology is nothing more than history garbled; likewise history is mythology garbled and it is nothing more in all the history of man." . . .
> "What are scenarios?" says Winifrede.
> "They are an art-form," says the Abbess of Crewe, "based on facts. A good scenario is a garble. A bad one is a bungle. They need not be plausible, only hypnotic, like all good art." (pp. 103–6)

The abbess, having chosen the truth of art above the truth of being, is clearly sailing to a destination like the Byzantium of Yeats. And sail she does at the end of the novel, though in the propemptikon (or godspeed wish) that forms its finale her destination is Rome. The author, for all the lyricism and delicacy of her envoi, implies that Alexandra is not likely to succeed in seducing the Inquisition as easily as she has seduced her nuns. Even Gertrude is forced to acknowledge this, sensing that the Church authorities, who bridge matter and spirit, sense and sensibility, will reject Alexandra's sophistries as they have her own:

> "Well," Gertrude says, "you may have the public mythology of the press and television, but you won't get the mythological approach from Rome. In Rome, they deal with realities." . . .
> "Gertrude, you know I am become an object of art, the end of which is to give pleasure."

"Delete the English poetry from those tapes," Gertrude says. "It will
look bad for you at Rome. It is the language of Cranmer, of the King
James version, the book of Common Prayer." (pp. 125–26)

The poetry of the prayer book is of course the standard plea
against liturgical reform within the Anglican Church, and it seems
as though Spark is drawing parallels between lobbies in that church
that attempt to freeze belief into decorative formularies unrespon-
sive to the dynamics of faith and similar Lefebvrian positions in
Rome. Whether they carry her endorsement is another matter entirely, and something about which the satire refuses to be definite.
The issue is complicated by the fact that, according to William
McBrien, "Spark is a member of the commission working on the
modernisation of the English Roman Catholic liturgy."[16]

The abbess may be heading for a sober encounter with the inquisition, but we take leave of her in the Trahernian world of childhood, where myth is the irradiating raison d'être. We might be all
too conscious of the deficiencies of her position and the inadequacy
of the calling that justifies it, and yet, like Gray in the *Eton College
Ode,* we feel reluctant to break the spell, since, for all its illusoriness, it
approaches what Barbara Keyser has termed a "vision of eternity."[17]
The spell, like the spell of the art into which the abbess has transformed herself, is truly hypnotic. However, even as the envoi from
The Tempest sounds, so does that cry from St. Peter, and the reader
is enjoined to be watchful in the midst of the trance—the world in all
its dangerous reality is poised to rush into the vacuum created by
the novel's feast of misrule:

Our revels now are ended. Be still, be watchful. She sails indeed on the
fine day of her desire into waters exceptionally smooth, and stands on
the upper deck, straight as a white ship's funnel, marvelling how the
wide sea billows from shore to shore like that cornfield of sublimity
which never should be reaped nor was ever sown, orient and immortal
wheat. (p. 128)

16. "Muriel Spark: The Novelist as Dandy," 172.
17. "Muriel Spark, Watergate, and the Mass Media," 153.

The Takeover
Vocation Misconceived

The antinomianism of the abbess of Crewe is contained by the Catholic Church, whose edicts she evades or distorts as the occasion requires. Insofar as she retains at least a nominal allegiance to Rome, she cannot properly be called a schismatic, though she comes close to being one on several occasions in the book. Spark's next novel, on the other hand, is more centrally concerned with schism and heresy. *The Takeover* traces the way in which a pagan cult is revived by a heresiarch who is short of cash, and who thus needs to make a profit quickly. His gulls are members of postwar society who, bored by its rationalist temper, are ready to embrace any non-Christian alternative to its humanism. As Velma Richmond has put it, "Modern man does not believe in God; nevertheless he is willing to believe not in nothing but in anything, and so cults are formed."[1] Vocation in these terms becomes not a calling to serve the transcendent other, but rather the edicts of a deified self. Spark's satire embraces not only the "priesthood" of Hubert Mallindaine, palimpsestically related to Father Socket and to Alexandra, but also the false vocations of those who are disoriented enough to welcome his cult and who have *voluntarily* submitted themselves to its specious discipline. (The nuns of Crewe, after all, were *required* by their vocation to be a dirigible flock of sheep, subject to the wills of Alexandra and Felicity in turn.)

In this respect *The Takeover* stands with *The Mandelbaum Gate* as the most wide-ranging of the novels in the canon, pointing in a frontal, almost prophetic way to deficiencies in society instead of exploring their local manifestations in the cliques of bachelors, schoolgirls, or hostel inmates that have often been the staple of

1. *Muriel Spark,* 142.

Spark's fiction. She even goes so far as offer an analysis of the oil crisis at one point, couched in the sort of language she usually reserves for the anagogic moments of her novels, when events of the narrative are put into Catholic perspective. This "takeover" by Arab economic power is one of the many meanings of the title, which include also the unlawful occupation of property and the cultural dispossession of Italy by the wealthy international set. But while a novel entitled *The Takeover* might seem to be about transition, it is as much about the immutability of change: a "takeover" that promises renovation (whether it be the irruption of Pentecostal beliefs and practices into the Roman Catholic Church, or Hubert's revival of pagan worship) proves in the long term to be nothing new. *Plus ça change, plus c'est la même chose.* These "innovations" simply arise from a desire for easy and superficial spiritual excitement (otherwise called sensationalism) that has existed since time immemorial.

The starting point of *The Takeover* is Frazer's description of the *rex nemorensis* in *The Golden Bough*. He was a priest of Diana at Nemi whose function could at any time be usurped ("taken over") by a stronger rival, and who had to guard his life in turn against potential usurpers. One sentence is worth special notice:

> The strange rule of this priesthood has no parallel in classical antiquity, and cannot be explained from it. To find an explanation we must go further afield. No one will probably deny that such a custom savours of a barbarous age, and, surviving into imperial times, stands out in striking isolation from the polished Italian society of the day, like a primaeval rock rising from a smooth-shaven lawn. It is the very rudeness and barbarity of the custom which allow us hope of explaining it. For recent researches into the early history of man have revealed the essential similarity with which, under many superficial differences, the human mind has elaborated its first crude philosophy of life.[2]

The simile of a primeval rock is one that Spark herself has used to describe an aspect of her vision, its aspect of concessive retraction, of "nevertheless":

> But the physical features of the place [Edinburgh] are surely as special as themselves upon the outlook of the people. The Castle Rock is something, rising up as it does from pre-history between the formal grace of the New Town and the noble network of the Old. To have a great primitive black crag rising up in the middle of populated streets

2. Sir James George Frazer, *The Golden Bough*, 1:2.

of commerce, stately squares and winding closes, is like the statement of unmitigated fact preceded by "nevertheless."[3]

The image in both writers is of the immitigable way in which an older system of values challenges a new. In *The Takeover*, materialists turn to paganism for the crude emotional stimulus it promises, and so the impulses denied by their rationalism are exercised in new and perverted ways. "Pre-history" intrudes on civilization, or, to use a theological language more appropriate to the earlier fiction, original sin infects the drive to evolution and matches technological advance with moral regression. In Spark's earlier view, succinctly rendered through such novels as *The Bachelors*, it is only through vocation to faith (not to synthetic, self-made cults) that a bulwark against that sin can be found. *The Takeover*, however, a successor and continuator of the "exilic" fiction, does not foreground this solution. Far from being vividly dramatized, it is accorded little space and is represented only by the marginal figure of Nancy Cowan.

The major characters continue in the folly of their ways like self-regenerating amoebae and seem even to earn grudging authorial admiration for their indestructibility. Gone is the providential coda of judgment and reward that in, say, *Memento Mori* spelled out the author's position in relation to her characters. And gone also are a certain clarity and decisiveness. Having spent so much time imagining people as worthless as those of *The Takeover*, the author seems herself to have succumbed to their ennui and moral listlessness. Human beings now seem incorrigible, and the "corrective" metaphysical framework that governed and shaped the early novels with such purposefulness has been dismantled. "Why break butterflies upon a wheel?" the implication seems to run. But that being so, why dignify butterflies with fictional treatment in the first place, if the norms of faith and satire—Spark herself has equated them—seem too weighty for the task in hand?

The first butterfly to flutter into sight is Hubert Mallindaine, whom we encounter obsessively measuring time:

> At Nemi, that previous summer, there were three new houses of importance to the surrounding district. One of them was new in the strict sense; it had been built from the very foundations on cleared land where no other house had stood, . . . and constructed, over a period of three years and two months ("and seven days, three hours

---

3. "Edinburgh-born," 180.

and twenty minutes," the present occupant would add. . . . . "I timed it. God, how I timed it!")

The other two houses were reconstructions of buildings already standing or half-standing; both had foundations of Roman antiquity, and of earlier origin if you should dig down far enough, it was said. Maggie Radcliffe had bought these two, and the land on which she had put up the third house.[4]

In this topographical description, as apparently neutral as an architect's report, is it possible to detect a glimmer of allegory. The "new" house will later be shown to be *abusivo,* its existence denied by legal fiction, as other tangible structures of belief are denied or ignored by protagonists in the book. The other houses, superimposed on existing foundations, supply an image of persistence, of regeneration ineradicably rooted in the decayed semblance of itself, as the rich assume the garb of paupers in order to protect their fortunes. Hubert's irritable consciousness of time shows him (like other members of the international set) incapable of conceiving the reality of eternal life. Spark will later celebrate this life in what John Updike has called a "stunning paean,"[5] presenting its permanence and immutability and showing how it makes risible the treasures that moth and rust corrupt.

Maggie Radcliffe, Hubert's chief adversary, has her verbs of being busily conjugated to suggest that she also moves exclusively within the realm of time, the focus of his chronocentric attention:

> Maggie herself was never there that previous summer, was reputed to be there, was never seen, had been, had gone, was coming soon, had just departed for Lausanne, for London.
> Hubert Mallindaine, in the new-built house, had news of Maggie; had seen, had just missed, Maggie; had had a long discussion with Maggie; was always equipped to discuss knowledgeably the ins and outs of Maggie's life. He had been for years Maggie's friend number one and her central information agent. (p. 6)

While this compendium of gossip-column phrases might suggest Maggie's social luster, it also conveys the goallessness of her life in a "multiple choice" of destinations, arrivals, and departures, all sharing parity with each other. Her friendship with Hubert is given a numerical rating, not an adjective of value, and is aligned with gossip and tale-bearing and with material quid pro quos.

4. Spark, *The Takeover,* 5. Henceforth cited parenthetically in the text by page number.

5. John Updike, "Seeresses," 170.

Claiming "descent" from the goddess Diana, Hubert demands special privileges, and Maggie Radcliffe at first concedes them to him without question, as though this lineage were something real. And so he moves into one of her houses with a large number of young men in tow. In the world of the rich and privileged, desire converts to need, mythology to unquestioned fact. Temporal power has the effect of making fantasy seem real. The "encampment" of Hubert in his legend suggests not only the insistence with which he advertises it, but also his sexual unorthodoxy—*encampment* encases the slang meaning of *camp*—a point immediately confirmed by the disconcertingly numerous harem of "secretaries" and the languor and oddity of their dialogue. Spark is no doubt implying that Hubert has that incapacity for stable relationships in which some homosexuals appear to take pride (another Roman exile, Gore Vidal, comes to mind). He later confesses his terror of permanence and faithfulness in terms that connect them to sexual perversity: "A bond . . . is not very far from bondage" (p. 108).

This emotional rootlessness parallels the *déraciné* lifestyle of Maggie Radcliffe, the internationalism of which is symbolized by a gallimaufry of languages and scraps of experience. Still, the temporal frame "at that time" suggests that the "liberty" of her uncentered mode of being has been called into question by the economic crisis in the background of the novel:

> She handed over the fretful details of the purchase of land and buildings at Nemi and had telephoned to Hubert from Rome in that special jargon used by people who at that time woke and took breakfast, as it might be, in Monte Carlo, flew to Venice for a special dinner, Milan next evening for the opera, Portugal for a game of golf and Gstaad for the week-end. "J'ai compris—toute à Nemi. . . . What do you mean, 'my policeman lover'. . . . Well, darling, he's handsome. I have to sleep with someone. . . . Va bene, va bene, Hubert, ma cosa vuoi, tu? I tuoi ragazzi." (pp. 96–97)

The ethos of the society in which Maggie moves denies the absolute value of commitment, whether it be to human being or to God, and it is handled with a tolerance at odds with the rigorous, even judgmental procedures of the early novels. Margaret Drabble has observed that "the book presents a glittering surface. . . . But . . . what lies beneath this dazzling game? Anything? Nothing? and, as ever, [Spark] leaves us on our own, for most of the book, to try to answer it."[6] The leisured rich who swarm across the pages of Spark's later

6. "*The Takeover*," 16.

fiction have little to believe in and little to do, as the presentment of Hubert at the end of Chapter 1 implies. He is like them in their ennui and lack of purpose, but, unlike them, he is poor. That is one reason for him to lay claim to a divine descent that "validates" the privileges he craves. He surveys his chances of getting these with Olympian dispassionateness, as if through the eyes of his "ancestor" the goddess Diana. Meditating on the possibility that Maggie might die in an airplane crash and so rid him of his financial worries, he pulls a hair from his beard as if to confirm the reality of pain (p. 8). The alignment of an air disaster and the extraction of a hair suggests the futility and idleness of the man and the way he trivializes the suffering likely to bring him accidental benefits. His is a lotos-eater mentality, incapable of immediate feeling. It is hardly surprising therefore that the religion he is about to found will turn on *self-induced* emotion, emotion induced to fill a vacuum of insentience. His cult will spring from a background of instability and world-weariness.

Spark emphasizes Hubert's passivity, as well as his readiness to exploit the realm of the spirit for financial gain. This is the point of the mental transition from a dreaminess that picks up Wordsworth's "Daffodils" (as if to parody that poet's delight in simple things) to Hubert's thoughts about hard cash: "He didn't quite know what to do. But he had one resource. Its precise application was still forming in his mind and wandering lonely as a cloud, and meantime he was short of funds" (p. 10). Whereas earlier we have seen him lay claim to the view of Nemi as a patrimonial right, here, in realizing that he can no longer afford the view, he encounters the financial realities that throughout the novel arraign the rich and force them to reconsider their unfounded sense of omnipotence. Paradoxical seesawings of this order are inherent in a life so given over to the pursuit of pleasure that it is reduced to an undirected round of sensations, tabulated with the same unmeaning exhaustiveness as Maggie's travels earlier in the novel: "He retained an inkling that the poetry was still there and would return. Wordsworth had defined poetry as 'emotion recollected in tranquillity.' Hubert took a tranquillizer, quite a mild one called Mitigil, and knew he would feel better in about ten minutes. To make sure, he took another" (p. 12). That Hubert is unable to respond to life spontaneously is apparent in his distorted recollection of the Wordsworth *Preface,* which speaks crucially of the overflow of *powerful feelings.* Any generous upwelling of emotion is beyond the soul of someone who regulates it chemically with Mitigil.

One might imagine that characters so obviously shallow and worthless as Hubert and Maggie might, as in, say, *The Bachelors,* be offset by finer spirits, or at least by characters who make some sort of effort to invest life with a meaning beyond the accumulation of physical pleasures. This is not how Spark proceeds in her later work, however. In an interview with Sara Frankel, she has expressed what one imagines is an ever-increasing impatience with priests,[7] an impatience which might account for her mordant account of Maximilian and Baudouin in *The Abbess of Crewe* and their successors in *The Takeover* (also Jesuits)—though we must bear in mind that even in an early novel like *The Bachelors* we find Ronald taking off a callow young cleric. As spokespersons for a Catholicism contaminated with worldly compromise, Maximilian and Baudouin give seminars in ecclesiastical stage management and demonology, while in *The Takeover* Fathers Cuthbert and Gerard center their lives on socializing and "ecology."

Whereas in the early Spark, especially the Spark of the short stories, the Church is invoked as the custodian of an absolute dogmatic truth, Father Gerard's studies in "ecological paganism" would seem to call that certainty into question. He is concerned to prove that the pagan customs nominally baptized at the time of their "takeover" by the Church have not been essentially altered—"primaeval rock rising from a smooth-shaven lawn"—and that this paganism, involving nature worship, is necessarily based on sound ecological practices. Spark implicitly condemns this flirtation with topical concerns in the name of religion. Gerard's grasp of the matter is superficial to say the least, and, in his efforts to affirm the relevance of Catholicism to the twentieth century, he distorts important dogma to accommodate alien beliefs. Perhaps because she sees the Church engaged in the undignified pursuit of the trendy and the ephemeral, Spark seems less and less able to invoke it as a stabilizing custodian of verities in her later work. Her earlier authorial imprimaturs and rejections now give way to cool, unvaluing transcriptions of corruptness. Unable to find a norm to govern the aim of her satire, she elects to target everything in sight and is often as much fascinated as repelled by what she satirizes. But there seems to be an additional strain of bitterness in her treatment of the Jesuits in this novel—the bitterness, possibly, of betrayal:

> "Priests," said Pauline. "They're terrorists. They hold you to ransom."

7. Frankel, "Interview," 446.

The Jesuits looked at each other with delight. This was the sort of thing they felt at home with, priests being their favourite subject. . . .

"What do you have against us?" Father Cuthbert said, shifting about with excitement in his chair as if he were sexually as much as pastorally roused. . . .

The younger priest sipped his drink and looked out over the still lake with its deep crater and the thick wildwood of Nemi's fertile soil. "Terrific ecology!" he said.

"You mean the view?" Pauline said. (pp. 15–16)

Hubert, as we have seen, regards commitment as a species of sadomasochism, and Gerard and Cuthbert resemble him, in this respect at least, by wriggling in a morbid way every time their commitment to the priesthood is called into question. On another occasion (pp. 107–8) they are presented as having greatly enjoyed Hubert's cooking, the view, and the insults he administers to their calling, titillated rather than roused to apologetics by his infidelity. At no point of the novel do they affirm any kind of religious orthodoxy. Indeed their lives are hedonistic and futile enough to bear comparison with Hubert's and Maggie's. Their vocation seems to have been reduced to sacerdotal narcissism—priests are their favorite subject of conversation—and the austerity of their calling swallowed up in their appetite for luxury and a meaningless social round.

The ineffectual pallor of the Anglicanism embodied by Father Childe in *The Girls of Slender Means* is now seen to have infected Catholicism as well. We are reminded of Joanna's lukewarm, worldly parent in the brief flashback to Hubert's childhood and his eccentric aunts. These women have also claimed descent from Diana, syncretizing their pagan cult with a feast of the Virgin Mary. They encounter no criticism from their vicar, however, who is all complaisant curiosity:

"It sounds most interesting," said the vicar . . . . [The aunts] were walking hand in hand, and his mother had finished explaining to the vicar that her sisters-in-law were convinced "Mallindaine" was a corruption of "maligne Diane." . . . "[The aunts are] on their way to Hampstead Heath; they do it every Lady Day," his mother said . . . . "They light a bonfire and offer up prayers to the goddess Diana, and I expect there are other rites. . . ."

"It sounds most interesting," said the vicar.

"I dare say it is most interesting," said his mother, "but it's embarrassing for me, because of the boy."

"Have they means?" said the vicar, gazing out on the sunny
Hampstead pavement. (pp. 94–95)

The vicar's reaction is of a piece with Father Gerard's to paganism,
the study of which he manages to combine with a touch of Maggie's
dolce vita:

> "I stayed with them, it was very comfortable. And I must say that area
> is rich in legends of nature worship. Mary listed for me many cases of
> surviving nature-practices and superstitions in that area. They're
> devout Catholics, of course. I'm not saying anything against their
> faith; those peasants are great Catholics."
> "But they worship the tree-spirits and the water-spirits," said
> Hubert.
> "No, no, I wouldn't say worship. You've got it wrong. The Church
> continues to absorb many pagan nature-rituals because the Church is
> ecology-conscious." (p. 105)

Well might one inquire what animism has to do with ecology, and
how its putative absorption by the Church can fuse essentially different views of God and His creation. Gerard paraphrases a per-
fectly reasonable objection in such a way as to evade it. It would
seem from this that essential differences are no longer upheld in the
Church and that its baptismal resolution to renounce the world, the
flesh, and the devil has become too intemperate to live with. Finding discretion the better part of valor, therefore, it has eagerly bade
them welcome. With Gerard and Cuthbert as exemplars of the priesthood, it is clear that the world has tainted the Church, and so the
Church can no longer stand in judgment on its futility.

Earnestness is not to be found in the Jesuit socialites, nor in the
indolent Hubert, nor in the frantic, hedonistic Maggie. Mary, her
daughter-in-law, does, however, try to impose a vocational pattern
on her life. Her leitmotiv is "success," a notion which she has raised
to the status of a creed. As so often in Spark, misplaced obsession is
rendered by the rhetorical figures of *heratio* and *traductio,* so that
"success" comes again and again with nauseating insistence throughout the passage:

> She was terribly anxious to make a success of her marriage, as she
> would put it; her father was a success and her mother a well-known
> success in advertising although she didn't by any means need the job;
> moreover, Mary's elder sister was busy making a success of her mar-
> riage. Mary had been successfully brought up, neither too much nor
> too little indulged. And so, still half under the general anaesthetic of
> her past years, Mary was not disposed to regard Maggie as critically as

she would have done had Maggie not been her mother-in-law; it was
part of making a success of her marriage. (pp. 48–49)

Mary is a distant relation of Henry James's ingenuous Americans,
trying to be honest in a dishonest milieu, though it says something
about the moral nihilism of Spark's "international theme" that "success" can seem to qualify as a value in the absence of any others.
Mary's recipe is based on conformation, on responding to people as
she perceives they want her to. Her will is thus misdirected into
sycophancy, always adjusting itself to the expectations of others,
and forfeiting all claims to truth and sincerity as it does so. We find
this in her echoic conversation with the mother-in-law whom "success" indemnifies from criticism in her eyes. Spark is clearly irritated by her double *very*, rhetorically excessive in the eyes of a
writer who loathes excess, and also disproportionate to the problem
it qualifies:

> "It's a problem."
> "It's a very, very big problem," said Mary, eager to be entirely with
> Maggie. "It's a tremendous problem."
> "And there's that lesbian secretary living with him," Maggie said.
> "Is she a lesbian?"
> "I guess so. What else would she be?"
> "I guess that's right," said Mary.
> "She couldn't be normal, living there with him."
> "Well, it could be platonic like when you were friends with him,"
> Mary said, "but I guess it isn't." (pp. 50–51)

Maggie—as she often does—is treating the conversation as a catharsis, saying things to vent her feelings rather than to utter truths. She
has no grounds whatever for calling Pauline a lesbian, apart from a
need to vent her rage in malice. Mary, taking a litmus test every step
of the way, manages "successfully" to concur, though she is aware
that the truth is being distorted. Spark hints at her callowness by
describing her past as a state of anesthesia and suggesting that
privilege and purposelessness have numbed her responses, as Hubert's Mitigil tablets have his. The compulsive lists that she draws
up, like her cult of success, are an immature attempt at imposing
order on a life that de facto can have none. She makes lists of
clothes, her housekeeping expenses, her letters, her library, and her
record collection, typing them from rough drafts, and then filing
them alphabetically or chronologically (p. 63). Order is being deified
in divorce from the substance ordered, and, in the absence of what

the Abbess Alexandra would call a destiny, Mary worships it as the handmaiden of success.

Maggie's answering obsession is with plans, no sooner made than broken, as if to confirm the false omnipotence with which her wealth has invested her. A letter she writes to Hubert thrums remorselessly on the word, and the reader is again alerted by the figures of *heratio* and *traductio* to be on guard against the character's foolishness: "I expect you too will have plans to go to the sea. . . . Berto . . . plans to join me on the Emerald Coast . . . . They plan to look over some horses he plans to buy. I plan to join him in Rome, then Nemi for a week on October first after which our plans take us back to the Veneto" (p. 81). This rhetorical harping on success and plans and lists is symptomatic of unease, and Hubert does indeed accuse Maggie of showing a hysterical desire for structure in an otherwise unstructured life (p. 83).

Mary's lists are her talisman against failure in marriage, a failure she is all too justified in dreading. However smoothly she may run her home and whatever her finesse as an organizer of dinner parties, her husband is an adulterer. The narrator informs us calmly and unjudgmentally that Michael has a mistress in Rome, a vice "not unusual" for Italian businessmen (p. 61), and then, with more than a touch of pity and hint of patronage, notes that Mary would have considered her marriage a failure (that dreaded alternative to "success") had she known. As indeed she ought, though the cool authorial voice seems to intone amusement at her "naive" expectation that husbands ought to honor their marriage vows. When infidelity becomes venial because it is "not unusual," we have entered a world in which absolute values seem to exert no power, and in which the author would appear to lack the energy or desire to invoke them.

No figure better exemplifies the conscienceless, heartless adaptability of the beau monde than Lauro, servant to Maggie, Berto, and Mary, seducer and seduced of all. The casualness with which Maggie accepts her husband's affair with Berto is of a piece with Spark's account of Michael's Roman mistress—she scarcely bats an eyelid (pp. 125–26). Her calm reaction is entirely typical of her world. Sexual appetite, like the appetite for holidays, or jewels, or paintings, is there to be gratified, not disciplined and redeemed by a context of love. Lauro is simply an adjunct of wealth, to be dispensed with once his purpose has been served. He comes in some ways to embody the Italy venally open to takeover by the international set, adjusting principle to material gain or, in an episode that

verges on allegory, burying the spoils of his thefts and of his pros-
titution in the family grave and yet winning respect for the apparently pious way in which he honors the memory of his parents.

Lauro's antitype is Letizia Bernadini, whom William McBrien
describes as "myopically left-wing . . . the cognate of Felicity in *The
Abbess of Crewe*."[8] She is chauvinistic and unreflecting, her national
pride a substitute for the Christianity that might otherwise have
centered her desire to believe in something:

> Letizia, a passionate Italian nationalist with an ardour for folklore and
> the voluntary helping of youthful drug-addicts, resented very much
> the fact that her father rented the house from an American. She was
> against the foreign ownership of Italian property, held that the youth
> of Italy was being corrupted by foreigners, especially in the line of
> drugs, and asserted herself, with her . . . large-boned athletic shape-
> lessness, and religious unbelief, to be a representative of the new
> young Italy. (p. 32)

The exclusivity of nationalism is scarcely to be preferred to Lauro's
self-seeking, for, even if it helps forge an identity, the result is essentially callow, making Letizia a variant of the Israeli guide in *The
Mandelbaum Gate,* with his boast of sellotape and cement factories
and his unconcern for the realm of the spirit. Since it traffics in
manageable reductions, her xenophobia fails to account for the
guilt and complicity of Italy's young men and women in their own
downfall. The behavior of Lauro calls her blatant, oversimple creed
into question, for there can be no doubting that he seeks out his own
corruption. Whereas he is endlessly opportunistic, endlessly mal-
leable, endlessly ready to compromise, Letizia exemplifies unyielding stasis, a condition which, in its different way, is quite as nasty.
She is caught up in attitudes that will prevent her developing and
evolving—her life between eighteen and forty-five, it is suggested,
will be an existential desert of sameness. This is clearly Joanna
Childe seen through the other end of the telescope, arrested by a
fatal limitation of creed, stunted by vocation misconceived.

Letizia's name means "joy," and yet her worship at the shrine of
nationalism is harsh and joyless; Lauro's implies the laurel of victory, and yet his worship of the self is undignified and contemptible.
No less contemptible are those—the whole of Maggie's acquaintance, in fact—who give credal form to their appetites. Their futile
efforts at formulating a religion of poverty and riches in the stock

8. "Muriel Spark: The Novelist as Dandy," 174.

markets, and founding it on journalistic scripture, cause the author to make a rare appearance in propria persona:

> They all understood these were changing in value . . . ; they habitually bandied the phrases of newspaper economists and unquestioningly used the newspaper writers' figures of speech. They talked of hedges against inflation, as if mathematics could contain actual air and some row of hawthorn could stop an army of numbers from marching over it. They spoke of the mood of the stock-market, the health of the economy as if these were living creatures with moods and blood. And thus they personalized and demonologized the abstractions of their lives, believing them to be fundamentally real, indeed changeless. But it did not occur to one of those spirited and in various ways intelligent people round Berto's table that a complete mutation of our means of nourishment had already come into being where the concept of money and property were concerned, a complete mutation not merely to be defined as a collapse of the capitalist system, or a global recession, but such a sea-change in the nature of reality as could not have been envisaged by Karl Marx or Sigmund Freud. (p. 127)

This is very much in the spirit of Gray's "Alas, regardless of their doom, / The little victims play!," a privileged authorial view on the obtuseness of her characters, a Cassandra cry in parenthesis. Here Spark dissolves the "reassuring" solidity of materialism, whether it be taken in its sense of worldly acquisitiveness or read with its philosophical meaning. The only concreteness she allows it is the concreteness of metaphor. To theologize economic success is to court the disaster that the prophetic aside foresees, confident in the predictions of the "Magnificat" that "the rich shall be sent empty away." Indeed the dizzying reversals of that canticle work themselves out through the plot of the novel. Rich people have to practice poverty to maintain their affluence or have to hire interlopers to keep interlopers at bay, as Maggie does at her house in Ischia. Her paradoxical complaint confirms the author's view: "'The time is coming,' Maggie said severely, 'when we'll have to employ our own egg-throwers to throw eggs at us, and, my God, of course, miss their aim, when we go to the opera on a gala night.' She had sighed; a deep sigh, from the heart" (p. 114). The irony is that this witticism unwittingly prophesies the course she will have to follow to recover her stolen fortune.

Spark conveys the undetectability of economic transformation through Ariel's image of sea-change, suggesting both engulfment and the inscrutable shades of difference that lead finally to an altered identity. It is an image that seems also to resonate with Maggie's necklace at the time of the first robbery:

> On her arms and around her neck she wore the jewellery she had put on for dinner: bracelets and long necklaces of sea-shells which she had taken the whim to have set by a jeweller in conjunction with rubies and diamonds. These jewels, which were now all the summer jewellery she had left, made a sound like little dolls' teacups being washed up in some toy kitchen as her arms waved and her mouth gasped.
> (p. 133)

Sea shells, as we know from the terminal image of *The Public Image*, function for Spark as motifs of beautiful vacancy, memorials of the life they once held. The shells of Maggie's necklace by the same token are products of the "sea-change" that has given them parity with diamonds and rubies, their reduced status as playthings fixed in the simile of dolls' teacups. This same jewelry later clanks like Marley's chain, suggesting both enslavement and a ghostly semblance of being (p. 137). Irony again comes into play as Maggie's instinctive sense that Coco has stolen her jewels, once proved to be false, prepares the way for his appropriation of her entire fortune. Mutatis mutandis, we have seen the same narrative strategy at work in *The Girls of Slender Means*, with its cry of "wolf" before the real cataclysm occurs. The immediate takeover of the jewels dovetails into the larger takeover of the fortune, which in turn is being taken over by that immaterial devaluation of the material that Spark has predicted in her long aside about Berto's dinner guests.

As Maggie's fortune begins to evaporate through mysterious transfers and embezzlements, she is possessed by the sense of panic that her obsessive "plans" have managed to keep at bay. It becomes apparent to her in the midst of her crisis that even Berto's love for her is not deeply rooted. The frail contact with reality that her endless telephone calls have guaranteed has been broken by a telephone strike, and her response, as poignantly futile as Marie Antoinette's to the crowd demanding bread, is to rattle her receiver for hours on end (p. 141). While she is thus engaged, she sees Berto going about his business on the estate, apparently immune to the panic and angst that have seized her. Suddenly she realizes that nothing will be altered by her death, that within days of immuring her body in the family vault, he will continue to consult his groom as he is consulting him now. There will be a standard funeral, a token appearance of the Italian nobility, and then her son will wind up her estate. That will be the only evidence of her having lived at all, so vapid and self-absorbed is her way of life. When Maggie sees her husband behaving as if the world were not ending, we assume the apocalyptic reference to be nothing more than the hyperbole she habitually uses. Then, remembering the author's grave prediction about the economic sea-change, we realize that the end of the world as she has known it is indeed about to occur. Even as Berto in his Audenesque way turns from her imagined funeral to resume his life, that life, apparently serene and unassailable, will have been altered beyond recognition. It is a poignant moment in the novel, the more poignant for being so quietly and briefly handled.

There, then, we have the social milieu into which Hubert is about to launch his cult of Diana, a milieu in which the seemingly immutable props of wealth and privilege are dissolving undramatically but relentlessly, and in which new sources of value are being investigated and adopted. At this point the novel recalls the "feast of misrule" atmosphere that suffuses *The Abbess of Crewe*. The "scenaristic" garble of Hubert's first sermon as priest of Diana makes this clear, as does the color of his vestments—green and white were also Alexandra's favorite shades:

> "Truth," said Hubert, "is not literally true. The literal truth is a common little concept, born of the materialistic mind." He raised his right arm gracefully from the lectern before him, and with it the sleeve of his green and silver . . . vestment. . . .
>
> "Brothers and sisters of Apollo and Diana," Hubert went on, with his eyes focused defiantly on Pauline, "we hear on all sides about the evil effects of inflation and the disastrous state of the economy. Gross materialism, I say. The concepts of property and material possession are the direct causes of such concepts as perjury, lying, deception and fraud. In the world of symbol and the worlds of magic, of allegory and mysticism, deceit has no meaning, lies do not exist, fraud is impossible. . . ." (p. 138)

Hubert, advancing his trivialized version of truth, seems to pick up at the point where Pilate left off, showing the same failure to recognize its legitimate, disinterested embodiment. The truth—that he cannot afford the house he is illegally occupying, that he is not in fact descended from Diana, that Diana herself never existed—is too uncomfortable to live with, just as the abbess of Crewe finds postconciliar Catholicism distasteful. Their solution is identical: define the intractable truth away and substitute an amenable fiction. Hubert's sermon is nothing more than *réchaufé* of the abbess's "realm of mythology" address. Both set forth a doctrine that turns the world into a human rather than a divine artifact, and so exempts it from the ethic imperatives that obtain in real life. Once one has entered the realm of fiction, one has entered a realm of pseudo-statements and can juggle these at whim, since they have been partly emptied of reference. Only the deranged—and Hubert himself courts madness when eventually he believes his own lies— would confuse the "deceit" of fiction with moral deceit. The first is inoculated by the acknowledged laws of art, while the deceit of a confidence trickster is based on concealing empirical truth rather than bracketing it. Joseph Hynes has noted how magic "and super-stition are snares because they try to satisfy the longing for 'the immaterial' by closing eyes to the rest of the real."[9] Eyes cannot be kept closed too long, however, or a collision with reality will occur. Problems do not vanish because they have been dematerialized by verbal definition, as Alexandra and Hubert learn to their cost.

Spark has repeatedly presented metaphysical health as a compound vision, one that acknowledges the reality of matter and at the same time moves through the material world to the spiritual one. Hubert, like Seton in *The Bachelors*, short-circuits matter in all its tangibility, and his purpose in doing so is identical: to evade the rigors of the moral life. The only difference is that Hubert—initially at least—is a conscious fraud and has to stare down the skepticism of Pauline Thin. His arguments throughout the sermon prove specious, paradoxes that are tactically airy and epigrammatic, so that any challenge to their truthfulness will be made to seem literal-minded or Philistine. It is the mode that Oscar Wilde exploited quite ruthlessly, and which allowed him to get away with a great deal. If, as Wilde claimed, nature imitates art, or if, as Hubert asserts, truth is not literally true, we dare not challenge the nonsense for fear of having reacted inappropriately to a light-hearted tone. No such misgiving need deter us from trouncing Hubert's Alexandra-esque sneers ("a common little concept" recalls the abbess at her most judgmental), for their snobbery is there for all to see. Having, like Alexandra, advocated an aesthetic world in which autotelic laws of art displace the laws of morality, he uses that suspension of judg-ment to license sin. Thus the way is cleared for the "takeover" of orthodoxy by heresy, of reality by self-projected fiction, of identity by inauthentic facsimile:

> "Truth," Hubert repeated as he wound up his sermon, . . . "is not literally true. Truth is never the whole truth. Nothing but the truth is always a lie. The world is ours; it is in metaphorical terms our cap-

9. *Art of the Real,* 125.

ital. . . . The world is ours to conserve, and ours are the fruits thereof to consume. We should never consume the capital, ever. If we do, we are left with the barren and literal truth. . . ." (pp. 148–49)

It is an old comic strategy to take abstract concepts and bend them to fit the concrete circumstances of the bender. In W. S. Gilbert's *Princess Ida*, for example, Lady Blanche conceives subjunctivity and tense in terms of her own ambition to run Castle Adamant: "Oh, weak Might Be! / Oh, May, Might, Could, Would, Should! / How powerless ye / For evil or for good!"[10] By the same token, Truth is an abstraction and has never had any pretention to being an empirical datum. Only in Hubert's distorted vision would it aspire to being "literally true"—and his vision is distorted because he has collapsed the world of existence into the world of art. There can be no doubting the fact that he fears the judgment of the world, so obsessively does he recur to the oath of the witness stand, dissecting it phrase by phrase and reconstructing it in artful and meaningless paradoxes. Whereas the people around Berto's dinner table had made a religion of acquisition by imposing a concrete reality on abstractions, Hubert's cult does precisely the opposite, allowing the real to evaporate in his economic and ecological parables. The pattern of thought is thoroughly but plausibly confused, and so meets the specifications for a good garble laid down by the Abbess Alexandra. Hubert's Rorschach blot of "capital" (does it imply the earth itself or the imagination untrammeled by empirical limits?) enables even Cuthbert and Gerard to find in it an echo of their current obsessions. They go so far as to give his cult a qualified blessing, arguing as skewly as Hubert himself that any religion is better than none. We must not forget, however, that the sect has been launched as a source of revenue for a man on the brink of poverty and that the "capital" of his discourse has therefore also a literal economic meaning. Self-seeking, as with everything else in the novel, proves in the last resort to be the "ruling passion."

Bacon's image of the spider schoolmen reminds us that truth cannot be generated from the self alone, but from the self in responsible relationship with the world, and it is this relationship that Hubert and Alexandra have abrogated. Dorothea Walker, no doubt with Hubert's sermon in mind, aligns him with Jean Brodie: "Like Miss Brodie, he is his world as she is hers. Each refuses to acknowledge a higher authority."[11] In the earlier novel, indeed, Spark sug-

10. Gilbert, *The Savoy Operas*, 230.
11. *Muriel Spark*, 81.

gests that Miss Brodie's spirit would have profited from the external disciplines of Catholicism:

> Her disapproval of the Church of Rome was based on her assertions
> that it was a church of superstition, and that only people who did not
> want to think for themselves were Roman Catholics. In some ways,
> her attitude was a strange one, because she was by temperament
> suited only to the Roman Catholic Church; possibly it could have
> embraced, even while it disciplined her soaring and diving spirit, it
> might even have normalized her. (pp. 112–13)

Nowhere in *The Takeover* does Spark say anything comparable,
probably because, with postconciliar Catholicism in the state it is,
no obvious source of discipline is apparent. What obsesses her
rather are the rampant Charismatics and the sniggering, socializing
Jesuits. Yet that aspect of Protestantism which licenses the soarings
and divings described in *The Prime of Miss Jean Brodie,* and which
so frequently leads to schism, is exemplified also by Hubert's religion
of Hubert.

Interleaved within the sermon is a section that charts the gradual
loss of Maggie's fortune, now entrusted to that other plausible fraud,
Coco de Renault. Like Hubert, Coco screens his mismanagement of
her finances with reckless generalities—meaningless, but having
enough of what Alexandra would term the internal consistency of
myth to withstand Maggie's scrutiny. Spark's simile, derived from a
creation legend, shows that Coco, once more like Hubert, is diviniz-
ing self-interest. She describes him as having produced a plan "so
intricate that it might have been devised primordially by the angels
as a mathematical blueprint to guide God in the creation of the
world" (p. 140). The takeover of Maggie's fortune extends also to
the furnishings that she has left with Hubert in the villa. Chairs and
paintings are being systematically displaced with copies so plausible that their fraudulence is not immediately noticed. The treatment
of these artifacts parallels Hubert's activation of a dead religion,
subtly replacing a once-vital set of beliefs with manufactured rep-
licas. He does not perceive the discrepancy between his cult of the
immaterial and his theft of material goods. Integration and irradia-
tion of the self, the notes of vocation in Spark's early novels, are
nowhere apparent, and the conception of truth has been reduced to
confident plausibility. Indeed, Hubert relies on his blatant confidence to ride out any opposition to his lies. Pauline Thin is aware
that the genealogy on which he has based his cult is a fraud, and yet
she is intimidated by his confidence from calling his bluff. His

imperiousness exacts belief, and the servile Jesuits, by accommodating that confidence, forfeit their own credibility in turn. As Spark observes in one of her epigrammatic asides, the "expert self-faker usually succeeds by means of a manifest self-confidence which is itself by no means a faked confidence. On the contrary, it is one of the few authentic elements in a character which is successfully fraudulent" (p. 147). She goes on to describe this fake "authenticity" in terms of its orgulousness, an odd but expressive word she might have picked up from *Troilus and Cressida,* and which in one of her short stories she even applies to London buses. It is this rampant and scornful pride, made phonetically impressive and even ogrelike by its archaic adjective, that enables Hubert to shout down the queries of truth. It is a touch Hubertian of Spark to find reality in an impulse that discards the real, but the truth of the claim is borne out by the narrative. The religion is carried by the personality of its founder, and not by its truth.

Real genealogies, as well as faked ones like Hubert's, can also be treated as though they have a special sanctity. The rich in *The Takeover* have similarly mythologized their heritage, even if they stop short of claiming to be born of the gods. At Berto's dinner table we find an old relation of his who insists on telling the company about the activities of the clan (p. 166). Spark compares her discourse with the tragedies of the Athenian dramatists, who also assumed that their audiences would be fascinated by variations on plots they already knew. Once again, it is the confidence of the speaker that compels assent, a confidence that ensures her speech will be hypnotic, and hypnosis, as we know from Alexandra, is the quality of great art. At the back of this, and at the back of Hubert's cult, is the sense that value is being imparted to the wrong things and that the accidentals of birth and privilege are being given a worth they do not deserve.

Spark now attempts to show us where true worth is to be found. While other people are trying to create personal systems of value, she draws our attention to an invisible but magisterial reality they ignore in all their futile, secular efforts. This is done in what Updike calls the paean to eternal life. It comes too late and is too self-contained to exercise any influence on the plot, but as a return to the decisive, gnomic manner of the early fiction it is more than welcome. The passage has the effect of an epiphany that has been cut adrift and left floating above the novel in search of a character to which to attach itself. There is no such character, however, and it remains the property of the author and of the reader she shares it with. Spark is aware that her cast is virtually unredeemable and that none is worthy of the vision. In structural terms, this passage balances her jeremiad about the oil crisis earlier in the book. There the analysis centered on the way in which material goods have been devalued by an economic revolution that has reformulated the very notion of wealth. This loss of material value is a *dematerialization*, however, and not to be confused with the *immateriality* of eternal life. Spark is careful to disjoin her version of this life from the cycle of human effort and the civilizations it creates, as well as from the more permanently cyclic rhythms of nature, which is where humanists and pantheists have located their versions of eternity:

> The two women were greeted occasionally by busy shoppers who passed and swept a glance, along with their smiles, at Agata's hard-done-by belly of shame, while the whole of eternal life carried on regardless, invisible and implacable, this being what no skinny craving cat with its gleaming eyes by night had ever pounced upon, no tender mole of the earth in the hills above had ever discovered down there under the damp soil, no lucky spider had caught, nor the white flocks of little clouds could reveal when they separated continually, eternal life untraceable and persistent, that not even the excavators, long-dead, who had dug up the fields of Diana's sanctuary had found; they had taken away the statues and the effigies, the votive offerings to the goddess of fertility, terracotta replicas of private parts and public parts, but eternal life had never been shipped off with the loot; and even the lizard on the cliff-rocks in its jerky fits had never been startled by the shadow or motion of that eternal life which remained, past all accounting, while Clara and Agata chattered on, tremendously blocking everyone's path although no one cared in the slightest that they did so. (p. 181)

One of the most interesting aspects of this episode is its apparent gratuitousness; it emerges out of nothing more significant than the gossip of two women, and of women who are in any case marginal to the plot of *The Takeover*. Yet that very gratuitousness is meaningful, imaging as it does the way eternal life is inseparably attached to the natural. All the time it runs alongside daily life, above and beyond its irrelevancies, but still providing the undeclared source of meaning. Orthodox Catholicism takes pains to distinguish between the two kinds of life, and, as so often in Spark, it is orthodoxy which inspires her to her best efforts. The following comes from a Catholic treatise that predates Vatican II:

> We possess in us, first of all, natural life, the life we receive from

our parents according to the flesh; by it we enter into the human family . . . .

But this natural life, *Ex voluntate viri, ex voluntate carnis* is not the only one. God . . . wills to give us a higher life which, without destroying the natural life in so far as it is good, surpasses it, upraises it and deifies it. God wills to communicate His own life to us.[12]

Spark's account of eternal life is preceded by a detailed description of life in Nemi on market day. Since it is a description of life *ex voluntate viri, ex voluntate carnis*, it is a description of contingent detail. The randomness of the catalog—the smithy, the fruit van, the electrician in his brightly colored car, the policeman, the town clerk, the Austin friar, the schoolboys—forms a poignant memorial to moments that will never be recovered from the passage of time, moments that have no meaning in relation to each other, moments unlinked by plot or causality. While she loves, and is moved by, these random secular details, Spark implies that their significance is not to be found in the contingent sequence in which they occur. It is eternity that attaches them to a pattern often imperceptible, but assented to by faith. The full meaning of these otherwise aleatoric events and people cannot be relayed because it is inexpressible in words. All Spark can do is state its nonequivalence with sensible items—cat and mole and clouds and artifacts of civilization—a ground bass supporting all of them, and conferring purpose where purpose is not immediately visible.

Of course the idea of two systems of experience, the natural and the supernatural, is a perennial one in Spark's fiction, but it has never been treated in quite this way before. Usually their coexistence is realized at the point of their intersection, especially in the short stories, where a divine phenomenon (for example the seraph on the Zambesi)[13] intrudes on a set of squalid, ordinary circumstances and offers the alternative of irresistible grace. Here, on the other hand, they are presented not as intersecting, but rather as running parallel. There is something deliberately prosaic and commonplace about the way eternal life is described as "going on," a flat, colloquial verb harnessed to a theological purpose. But that is precisely the point: Spark wants us to regard eternal life as something so incontrovertible and "present" that it can be described with a "meanwhile back at the ranch" formula. The "going on" also

12. The Right Reverend Columba Marmion, *Christ, the Life of the Soul: Spiritual Conferences*, 153–54.
13. "The Seraph and the Zambesi," in *Collected Stories I*, 112ff.

suggests the impersonal, unarrestable power of a divine purpose—adjectives such as *regardless* and *implacable* and *persistent* confirm this potency, which is intensified also by the fact that the participants in the natural life beneath it are to a creature unconscious of its existence, let alone its might. Because "eternal life" is mysterious and removed as it overshadows human activity, it can be apprehended only through grace, and cherished only through faith. Vocation is perhaps another name for that understanding, to be distinguished in its inscrutability from the manufactured vocation at the heart of Hubert's cult.

As the action of the novel advances, we find that his confidence has canceled his sense of reality and reduced him to abject belief in his self-made superstitions. Many of Spark's superstitious characters—Dottie in *Loitering with Intent* comes to mind—regard religion as an extension of the individual will, the subordination of God's purpose to a private plan secured by such formulas as the novena for the conversion of England.[14] Hubert is recognizably one of this company, since his faith, in addition to having flawed roots in fantasy, bases itself on the manipulation of God and humankind alike:

> Hubert did not know this, and in fact he had got into a habit of false assumptions by the imperceptible encroachment of his new cult; so ardently had he been preaching the efficacy of prayer that he now, without thinking, silently invoked the name of Diana for every desire that passed through his head, wildly believing that her will not only existed but would certainly come to pass. Thus, like ministers of any other religion, he was estranged from reality in proportion as he mistook the nature of prayer, offering up his words of praise, of gratitude, penitence, intercession and urgent petition in the satisfaction that his god would reply in kind, hear, smile, and wave a wand. So that, merely because he had known in the past that the unforeseen stroke of luck can happen, and that events which are nothing short of a miracle can take place, Hubert had come secretly to take it with a superstitious literalness that the miraculous may happen in front of your eyes; speak the word, Diana, and my wish shall be fulfilled. Whereas, in reality, no farmer prays for rain unless the rain is long overdue; and if a miracle of good fortune occurs it is always at the moment of grace unthought-of and when everybody is looking the other way. (p. 204)

Hubert's prayer manqué picks up the words of the centurion

14. *Loitering with Intent*, 130.

(Matthew 8:8)—"speak the word only, and my servant shall be healed" —words which are also used in the rite of the Mass. In their proper context, however, they are prefaced with a statement of humility: "Lord, I am not worthy." All this is subverted in Hubert's prayer to Diana. Whereas the centurion abased the self and made a disinterested request for the healing of his servant, Hubert is simply advancing the self, a self puffed up with its newfound powers. It is again possible to detect that recurrent hint of Auden's "Musée des Beaux Arts." Spark employs the turning away as a signature of grace, implicitly referring to such unspectacular aspects of the Incarnation as nativity in a stable or childhood in a carpenter's shop, moments of transfiguration that do not rely on publicity and self-advertisement. Upon this issue of publicity she founds part of her criticism of the Charismatic Revival, which she also connects with Hubert's religion. Those claims of individual illumination that were travestied in the abbess are again raised by this new infiltration into the Roman Church. It is described quite neutrally on p. 209 for the benefit of readers otherwise unacquainted with a phenomenon that entered Catholicism from Protestant sources in 1967. The tone is sharper and more hostile on other occasions, however, and one is never quite sure, as in *The Abbess of Crewe*, whether the derisiveness is authorial or not. Hubert, far from conceiving Pentecostals as possible schismatics from Rome, sees in their claims—as Spark herself seems to see—a thirst for that rather facile ecstasy and ready-made fellowship that his own cult offers: "It infuriated him to think of the crowds of charismatics in St. Peter's Square, thumbing their guitars, swinging and singing their frightful hymns while waiting for the Pope to come out . . ." (pp. 206–7). If Spark is also infuriated by what she sees, it is for very different reasons. Hubert simply thinks of the numbers as so many souls (and so much cash) lost to his cause. When he holds a festival of Diana at Nemi, the concourse is presented as a parody of Charismatic worship, with the same fervor and ecstatic public testimonies. Not surprisingly, it issues in riot, and in the fracas, Nancy Cowan, that marginal spokesperson for Catholic orthodoxy, literally defrocks Hubert by tearing off his vestments. Like Maggie, however, he proves indestructible, emerging phoenixlike from the ashes to be assimilated by Catholicism as an official Charismatic and also, no doubt, as an honorary ecologist. She herself recovers her fortune from Coco de Renault by kidnapping and blackmail, enacting, as she dons her costume of emblematic poverty, her prediction about hired egg-throwers for gala nights.

The Takeover, like *The Mandelbaum Gate*, loses thematic momentum before it concludes—the energy escaping in this case immediately after the dismantlement of Hubert's cult. The motors cut out, and the novel glides elegantly but listlessly to the ground. As before, length is partly to blame, primarily because Spark's bent in fiction is to summarize her material aphoristically and then to illustrate it, not to draw her meaning slowly from gradations of plot. Patricia Stubbs has criticized her for "her refusal to be committed, to solve her fictional situations, . . . her readiness to abandon all for a jest, . . . her random satire."[15] But to do so is to misunderstand her epigrammatic procedures and to judge her by the yardstick of novelists more ample in their methods. Proof may be found here, as elsewhere, that when she overextends her length, her novel runs out—of breath as much as of material. But that is only part of the dissatisfaction one feels on closing this book, as elegant and as trenchant as any written after *The Mandelbaum Gate*. The voice of judgment is too muffled, the treatment of worthless characters too lax to carry the prophetic indictment it sets out to make. When the old *furor poeticus* does flare out in the commentary on the oil crisis, or in the discourse on eternal life, one welcomes the zeal and energy it activates. But the glow of feeling at these rare visionary junctures, far from imparting their warmth to the novel as a whole, seems rather to show up the lassitude and indifference that appear to have so often overcome the author. One does not have to look beyond the cast of characters to find the source of the infection.

15. *Muriel Spark*, 33.

Conclusion

The connection between Muriel Spark's conversion and her self-discovery as a writer has marked her work indelibly. Vocation in her own life has forged her authorial identity and supplied her with a theme to which she could resort in novel after novel. In this study I have attempted to trace its recurrence in widely differing books from different phases of her career. Even so, it would be a mistaken view of the writer that failed to detect shifts in, and adaptations of, the perennial concern.

Spark's first novel, *The Comforters*, shows a certain reluctance in the convert, who must wrestle with the more repulsive aspects of Catholicism. To someone of discriminating taste, oleographs of the Sacred Heart, for example, or mass-produced plaster statuettes must have proved a trial of the spirit, and one can sense the artist's revenge in *The Comforters* when such devotional images are smashed by smugglers. But aesthetic afflictions of this order pale beside the ordeal of Georgina Hogg and all her idolatrous piety. Only recently has the Church of Rome acknowledged salvation outside itself, and it takes no effort of imagination to conceive its smugness and insularity at the time of Caroline's (and Spark's) conversion. None the less, the heroine of *The Comforters* finds her vocation as writer and believer by struggling to meet each and every demand orthodoxy places upon her. Caroline's religion is anything but a comfort; it has been adopted by reasonable decision, not by a leap of faith; it has to be honored by total obedience, not filtered to suit the inclinations of the believer.

In this unyielding rigor is an aspect of the author's vision that some of her detractors find hard to accept. Such critics, viewing the novels in humanist terms, have been repelled by a discipline that subordinates individual desire to the immutable (and often exorbitant) demands of dogma and have regretted its entrenchment at the expense, say, of Caroline's and Barbara's sexual happiness. And

135

here lies a rub that any admirer of Muriel Spark must address—the extent to which her beliefs impair the access of a non-Christian reader to her work.

We can take Patrick Parrinder as a spokesperson for humanist readers when he observes that Spark "is a notoriously anti-humanist novelist, who ultimately puts down a large proportion of the manifestations of human nature that she displays to the ragings of the devil."[1] Humanism is a highly problematic term, with almost as many significations as adherents. A unifying tenet behind its many forms, however, is that human beings create their own values, organize their own lives, and are responsible in these fields to no supernatural agency. But the "manifestations of human nature" to which Parrinder refers are often evil ones, and, within the Catholic frame of the novels, an aetiology of evil that traces them to original sin and, beyond that, to "demonic ragings" is (to say the least) internally consistent. And even if the humanist were to reject the mythological framework in terms of which, say, Selina's retrieval of the dress is placed, it is hard to see how those unlovely "manifestations" would prove less belittling of human dignity if they were derived from within the personality. One would imagine, on the contrary, that "undivinized" self-worth, which the humanist claims to celebrate, would better be served by the transfer of the guilt than by its absorption. The fact is that humans seldom conform to humanists' visions of their worth and dignity. Deny the Pelagianism on which ideas of *moral* progress and evolution are founded, as deny it one must when contemplating such twentieth-century horrors as the Holocaust, and the humanist is confronted with a problem of evil as insoluble as the problem of pain to orthodox believers. Both theist and antitheist positions are based on tenets of faith, and one person's "demonic raging" is another person's "human manifestation." As Browning's Bishop Blougram notes, "All we have gained then by our unbelief / Is a life of doubt diversified by faith, / For one of faith diversified by doubt: / We call the chess-board white,—we call it black." An obvious response to Parrinder's criticism, then, is to ask him to make the necessary imaginative adjustments, adjustments of the same order as those demanded, say, by *Mansfield Park* when it presents home theatricals as something indecent. If only for the sake of the imaginative vivacity with which they invest Spark's fictional world, those "ragings of the devil" must

---

1. Patrick Parrinder, "Muriel Spark and Her Critics," 25. Hereafter cited parenthetically in the text by page number.

be accepted as a datum, indeed as one of its empowering premises. In much the same way, Dante's *Divine Comedy* would fail to be, let alone mean, if one were to deny him his spatial conceptions of Hell, Heaven, and Purgatory. Whether or not one actually assents to Spark's extraliterary tenets, they have to be acknowledged with suspended disbelief if the works are to function according to plan, for it is through them that the writer's mythopoeic energies are canalized.

This goes some, but not all, of the way to addressing the problem Spark poses for readers who cannot assent to her vision. Usually, when dealing with writers of eccentric or untenable convictions, the humanist separates the ethical content from the supernatural, which is either winnowed away or tolerated for its fantastic charm. Matthew Arnold, for example, tries to distinguish the moral from the mythic content of religion in the following terms:

> It is exactly what is expressed by the German word "Aberglaube," *extra-belief*, belief beyond what is certain and verifiable. Our word "superstition" had by its derivation this same meaning, but it has come to be used in a merely bad sense, and to mean a childish and craven religiosity. With the German word it is not so; therefore Goethe can say with propriety and truth: "*Aberglaube* is the poetry of life,—*der Aberglaube ist die Poesie des Lebens.*" It is so. *Extra-belief*, that which we hope, augur, imagine, is the poetry of life, and has the rights of poetry.[2]

What cannot be believed by the humanist can at least be enjoyed as a discrete poetic experience. If one were to apply this to Spark, treating the religious dimension of the novels *only* as an imaginative resource, one could accuse her of favoring romance above realism. But any such accusation would be most unjust. Critics like Joseph Hynes have taken great pains to show that while the novels are not realistic in a traditional way, they are realistic in another. What Arnold would bracket off as *Aberglaube* cannot be detached from Spark's fiction without damage to its primary statements. Religion provides the underpinning of the characters' ethical conduct and, ultimately, the aesthetic conduct of the writer. Any dichotomous response must finally be inappropriate to a novelist bent on affirming the integral connection of theory and practice, of spirit and matter. One cannot sift and winnow, one must swallow whole. The imaginative effort Spark demands of the reader is not comfort-

2. *Literature and Dogma*, 58. Hereafter cited parenthetically in the text by page number.

ably selective, but rather one that honors the totality of her vision. Clearly, then, any would-be apologist must adopt a different strategy and prove to skeptics that the Catholicism does not impair so much as enhance the best of her work.

We need first of all to establish the fact that the religious beliefs that permeate the novels do not de facto render them illiberal, and therefore inaccessible to humanist readers. Let us return to Parrinder, who claims that the "author of *The Bachelors* (1960) was plainly no friend to practitioners of abortion, contraception, or homosexuality" (p. 26). Even if we leave aside his assumption that Spark is hostile (the tone of the novel is far more detached than he allows), we have still to ask ourselves whether someone who rejects the practitioners thus listed is *necessarily* antihumanist. Abortion can plausibly be defended as an entrenched right of women, but it can with equal plausibility be attacked for the way it devalues the sanctity of life, that tenet so central to a humanist vision of things. By the same token, while any automatic condemnation of homosexuality would justify charges of intolerance, one might ask whether those apologists for Gay Liberation who claim that fidelity and monogamy are the oppressive legacy of heterosexuals, and who urge promiscuity as a homosexual norm, ought to be honored as proponents of human worth and dignity. Is Father Socket condemned in *The Bachelors* because he is a homosexual, or because his idea of human relations is defective? Is it not truer to say that his inversion is presented as a metaphor of sterility? Notions of licence, while they might seem to validate human freedom, can at the same time debase it by subtracting the disciplines that give it form.

The fact remains, however, that institutions and values claiming divine imprimatur, especially institutions and values as confident and inflexible as those of the Roman Church, have been treated with caution and even disgust by contemporary humanists. Most of them do not manage the synthesis of Christian and pagan systems their sixteenth-century prototypes forged, but instead take antitheism as the foundation of any belief in human autonomy and worth. This is not the place to debate the validity of metaphysical systems, and I bring up the apparent conflict between Christianity and humanism only because it is prone to influence one's response to novels that, like those of Spark, unapologetically declare their Catholic allegiance. The better works in the canon, however, far from positing a theism hostile to humanist claims, often stress the way in which central humanist assumptions (like that of the dignity of humankind) are rooted in Christianity.

Spark's position would seem to be that of Henri de Lubac, who sees in patristic theology all those tenets "rediscovered" by the Renaissance:

"Man, know thyself!" Taking up, after Epictetus, the Socratic *gnôthi seauton*, the Church transformed and deepened it, so that what had been chiefly a piece of moral advice became an exhortation to form a metaphysical judgment. Know yourself, said the Church, that is to say, know your nobility and your dignity, understand the greatness of your being and your vocation, of that vocation which constitutes your being. Learn how to see in yourself the spirit, which is a reflection of God, made for God.[3]

This fervid rhetoric might seem far removed from the sober, chastened mode of *The Bachelors,* but it is nevertheless on such foundations—essentially humanist—that the characterization of Ronald Bridges is based. The temper of the twentieth century, from which Spark cannot (and need not) dissociate herself entirely, might make one cautious about de Lubac's vision, but one is not *bound* to reject its headiness for the futile cries of a Vladimir and an Estragon. Spark finds the automatic despair of the nihilist as dogmatic and unreflective as the buoyancy of the most unthinking humanist, and she gives Ronald no rein when he is tempted to it. Even at his most embittered and disillusioned, he turns for psychic renovation to an epistle by St. Paul, purifying the intractable fact of evil with the undeniable fact of good. However far removed her fictional economy and ironic mode might be from the nineteenth-century novelist's, Spark would, I am sure, agree with de Lubac when he claims that Dostoevsky "made one profoundly social truth clear: man cannot organize the world for himself without God: without God he can only organize the world *against man*. Exclusive humanism is inhuman humanism" (p. ix).

Many contemporary writers and philosophers, however, would disagree. E. M. Forster's is perhaps one of the more moderate voices that have been raised in objection to the purported antihumanism of religious belief:

My attitude towards religion may seem to such people very foolish. I like, or anyhow tolerate, most religions so long as they are weak, and I find in their rites an acknowledgement of our smallness which is salutary. But I dread them all, without exception, as soon as they

3. *The Drama of Atheistic Humanism*, 3. Hereafter cited parenthetically in the text by page number.

become powerful. All power corrupts. Absolute power which believes itself the instrument of absolute truth corrupts absolutely. Why shouldn't it? To take some examples; nothing could be more sensitive, cultivated and understanding than Roman Catholicism in an English University, where it must expect competition. Roman Catholicism in Ireland, where it is strong and unchecked, is a very different matter . . . .[4]

At first glance this seems reasonable enough, but it does not take long for us to hear the echo of Freddy's "absurd" in much of what Forster is saying. Like Freddy in *The Mandelbaum Gate,* he has totally misunderstood the nature of belief. This is not something that can be regulated by a spiritual rheostat to the desired level of tepidity, but rather a response made in conviction. In its classic definitions from Tertullian to Kierkegaard, faith is the feeling embrace of paradox and is predicated on the believers' readiness to lose themselves in an *O Altitudo!* Even Matthew Arnold, starting from Forster's rationalist premises, and like him ready to aestheticize religion into a beautiful, nonreferential body of thought, acknowledges that "the true meaning of religion is thus, not simply *morality,* but *morality touched by emotion*" (p. 16). In Forster's terms, on the other hand, any sort of commitment, not only the extreme of fanaticism, is a *necessary* source of corruption. But if this were so, there would be no translation of the realm of belief into the realm of action. Faith is compulsion; it brooks no argument. As Spark has said in an interview, "I couldn't believe anything else. It didn't particularly appeal to me: it still doesn't, but I'm still a Catholic. If I could believe anything else, I would."[5] If religion did no more than caution against pride and offer other "salutary" conducements to a sense of our smallness, the world would not have known St. Francis of Assisi or a Mother Teresa. Nevertheless, Forster's vision of religious feeling, based in turn on Arnold's, has widespread currency today. Religion in the West—the Middle East is a different case entirely—has lost the power to exact passionate allegiance.

By the same token, novels like those of Spark, which are rooted in the issues of Christian faith, must seem increasingly strange in the context of contemporary fiction. Here atheistic assumptions prevail—the result of the modernist legacy, and its attendant suspicion of teleological design. If the apologist cannot persuade a potentially hostile reader that the novels require imaginative assent to their

4. Quoted in Margaret Knight, *A Humanist Reader from Confucius to Bertrand Russell,* 155.

5. Gillham, "Keeping It Short," 412.

informing faith, then arguments conducted on aesthetic rather than theological grounds might carry the day. For it seems to me that the very originality of Spark's achievement can be traced to the un-shambling, unashamed way in which, in her early novels at least, unfashionable attitudes are firmly underwritten by the fiction. And, as I hope to show, the novels draw strength from the suppletive force of the dogma that underpins them. This strength, moreover, is a humanist strength insofar as it guarantees the worth and dignity of the characters in the narratives. Indeed it is when the Catholi-cism is dismantled (or rather occluded) in such apparently secular and antihumanist efforts as *The Driver's Seat* that Parrinder's charges begin to stick. We cannot blame Spark's Christianity for impairing the humanist value of her later fiction. It is much more the fault of her decision to embrace the neutralizing, even belittling, procedures of the *nouveau roman* and the Theater of the Absurd.

As I have repeatedly pointed out in the course of this study, Spark's doctrinal tenets are more fully manifest in the novels up to and including *The Mandelbaum Gate* than they are in their suc-cessors, and I would submit that they often (but not always) validate and dignify the works in question. Whether the reader assents to the informing Catholicism is not the point; what matters is the intensity and conviction of the author's recourse to that body of doctrine. Wilbur Sanders, writing of a religious poem by Donne, says some-thing important in this regard: "The theology is appealed to as if it were *there*; and thus, for the reader, it is there. This is the very antithesis of self-conscious play."[6] In the Introduction I drew atten-tion to the author's epigrammatic mode and to the deliberate excis-ions, distancings, skirtings, abridgements, tidyings, and capsula-tions that this entails. Human beings, placed on a Procrustean bed of epigram and seemingly trimmed of various freedoms to make them fit, would provide an unedifying spectacle were it not for the fact that a compassionate, "providential" attitude is governing the process. Caroline's retreats are presented as a duty necessary for her spiritual integration; she has no option but to undertake them. If this were not the case, the encounters with Georgina Hogg would lose their point—they would seem the sadistic manipulations of an author who, like the wanton boys in *King Lear*, has chosen to pull the wings off flies. And for a humanist critic, unwilling or unable to give imaginative assent to this assumption, Spark must often seem

6. *John Donne's Poetry*, 150.

just that. For example, Ruth Whittaker says of *The Mandelbaum Gate*:

> Barbara's quest for freedom from the confines of religious and political structures is reflected in [its] form . . . , which is much longer and closer to a "loose baggy monster" than any of the novels preceding it. It is as near to a "humanist" novel as Mrs. Spark ever gets, and in it she allows her characters much more freedom of choice than usual. This in part accounts for its length: options are offered by the author and explored by the characters and there is a sense of genuine alternatives.[7]

Such statements are presumably based on Barbara's admission that she would have continued her affair with her fiancé even if the Church had *not* dissolved his former marriage. If they are, they will not bear much scrutiny. For someone whose belief is so profound that it courts the possibility of death (Barbara goes on with her pilgrimage to Jordan, realizing the risk it poses to herself as a half-Jew), this resolve to continue the affair must be taken rather as a reckless kind of spiritual heroism, a kind prepared to accept that the world (not this world, but the next, in which she unwaveringly believes) is well lost for love.

Something comparable can be found in another Catholic novel, Graham Greene's *The Heart of the Matter*. Here is the scene in which Scobie's suicide is discussed by his widow and priest:

> "And at the end this—horror. He must have known that he was damning himself."
> "Yes, he knew that all right. He never had any trust in mercy—except for other people."
> "It's no good even praying . . . ."
> Father Rank clapped the cover of the diary to and said, furiously, "For goodness sake, Mrs. Scobie, don't imagine you—or I—know anything about God's mercy."[8]

Only in the context of an active faith can the tragedy of Scobie and the potential tragedy of Barbara Vaughan be actuated. Without that framework, the actions of each become nugatory (and even meaningless). At the same time, the orthodoxy of these characters is no abject submission, but a Jacob-wrestle with difficulties and unalterable demands. Their Catholicism provides aesthetic as well as moral strength. It supplies immutable coordinates for the graph of human aspiration, which has strenuously to conform to the claims of dogma

7. *Faith and Fiction*, 78.
8. *The Heart of the Matter*, 296.

and ethics. A system in which the participants make their own rules or modify them as they proceed is altogether less exacting, however liberating it might at first seem. Even so, viewed from a humanist perspective, the formulary nature of dogma will often seem tyrannical. Fixed belief is here being measured by a creed essentially relativist, even amorphous. As Geoffrey Heawood observes:

> No one would wish to indulge in a *tu quoque*; but it is a point that members of the churches are marked men and women. A trivial sermon, an ecclesiastical error of judgement or failure in charity, a conservative clinging to unscientific concepts, can be used to damn a whole body of Christians. Humanists have no institution, and therefore no corporate failings. It is well![9]

Because humanists have no institution, there is nothing to monitor slippage and adjustment when ideals become too difficult to live by. When, on the other hand, ideals persist in all their unalterability, their intemperate demands require the bravery of a Barbara Vaughan, whose faith embodies the "something greater" that Jacques Maritain advances as the frame of Christian humanism:

> Can man only come to know himself, in terms of renouncing the sacrifice of that self before something greater? . . . Certain forms of heroism would perhaps provide a solution of the apparent contradiction. Communist heroism claims to do so by the tension of revolution and the titanism of action, Buddhist heroism by pity and inaction. Another heroism claims to do so by love. The example of the humanist saints, the admirable Thomas More for instance, is from this point of view particularly significant. But does this example witness only to the fact that humanism and sanctity can co-exist, or also to the fact that it is possible to have humanism fed from the heroic springs of sanctity? Is there a humanism free and conscious of itself, which leads man to sacrifice and to a greatness which is truly superhuman, because here human suffering opens its eyes and endures its pain in love,—not in the renunciation of joy, but in a greater thirst, a thirst which is already joy's exaltation?
>
> Is a heroic humanism possible?[10]

His answer to his own question is, like Spark's, a guarded "yes," so long as the definition of humanism honors its Christian foundations.

I do not mean to claim that the Catholicism of Spark's early fiction inoculates it against trivial lapses, or passages of glibness, or

9. *The Humanist-Christian Frontier*, 16.
10. *True Humanism*, xiii-iv.

any number of cognate faults. On the contrary, the fault of doing too much too quickly impairs one or two works in this as much as in later phases of the author's career. Even in these slighter books, though, the dimension of faith adds a resonance to material that would otherwise seem impoverished by the very facility of its handling. In *Robinson,* for example, a novel too loose and contingent in its allegorical method to be called successful, there are some interesting instances of the heroism that orthodoxy sometimes demands. Where Defoe's Robinson Crusoe devoted all his wits to crafting the amenities of civilization, January Marlow, in her efforts to defend Mariology against the heterodox Robinson, improvises a rosary from beads that have been washed ashore. This earnest struggle to conform to the creeds and practices of the Church, and the way in which such orthodoxy is to some extent presented as a precondition for any fullness of being, persists through all the novels up to and including *The Girls of Slender Means.*

Spark's Catholicism in the early novels also provides moments of mystic illumination that shine forth and vanish as swiftly as they appear, epiphanies that Joyce would have rendered in secular terms, but which are offered here as moments of beatitude, irradiating the world with energy and purpose. One such moment can be found at the end of *The Ballad of Peckham Rye.* Although it has figured briefly in the discussion of *The Mandelbaum Gate,* it is worth reconsidering here as we try to assess the extent to which Spark's beliefs do not limit, but enrich, her early fiction:

> Humphrey drove off with Dixie. She said, "I feel as if I've been twenty years married instead of two hours."
> He thought this a pity for a girl of eighteen. But it was a sunny day for November, and, as he drove swiftly past the Rye, he saw the children playing there and the women coming home from work with their shopping-bags, the Rye for an instant looking like a cloud of green and gold, the people seeming to ride upon it, as you might say there was another world than this.[11]

The Ballad of Peckham Rye is a novel about a working-class suburb, a topic that would ordinarily require the methods of a Zola. If such moments never occur in social realist works, that is because the tradition is based on materialist premises. Spark, on the other hand, is under no such constraint. Here she can switch from a marriage obviously foredoomed to bitterness, presumably with its own cycle

---

11. Spark, *The Ballad of Peckham Rye,* 202.

of shopping bags and crossings of the Rye, to the transcendence available to all who are prepared to look for it—and Humphrey, after all, is looking in this particular instance. The people on the Rye are not angelic beings, they are laden shoppers, they seem only to ride like Hopkins's windhover—in fact they are probably trudging—but the ordinariness has been taken up into the transfiguration, not censored. By the same token, the green and gold that Dylan Thomas made the colors of an innocent and sacramental childhood in "Fern Hill" are also the real colors of grass in November sunshine, and behind the prosaic detail is the "rapture" passage in I Thessalonians 4:17: "Then we which are alive and remain shall be caught up together with them in the clouds, to meet the Lord in the air: and so shall we ever be with the Lord." Vision of this order, undemonstrative, unstrident, yet decisive in the way it is embodied, can be put alongside the final paragraph of *Wuthering Heights*, which is doing the same thing in reverse—offering pantheistic peace instead of theologically orthodox damnation: "I lingered round them, under that benign sky; watched the moths fluttering among the heath and hare-bells; listened to the soft wind breathing through the grass; and wondered how anyone could ever imagine unquiet slumbers, for the sleepers in that quiet earth."[12] What is so moving about both episodes is the way in which the authors enlarge the vision and augment the sonority by offering alternatives to more conventional assessments. In the case of Spark, Catholicism is underwriting the amplitude, and it would be an ungenerous reader that failed to acknowledge this.

The *Mandelbaum Gate* (more than any other novel in the canon) is filled with epiphanic moments, as Chapter 3 of this study has shown. It is also, sadly, the last to depend upon them in any significant way. (There is the "eternal life" passage in *The Takeover*, for example, but it owes its radiant conspicuity to the fact that it stands alone in the novel.) After Barbara Vaughan's inward struggle has been resolved, and the author's own struggle vicariously resolved through it, Spark begins to drift away from "heroic," rigorous conformity toward a stance of self-determination within the Church. It would not be an exaggeration to say that, with the completion of *The Mandelbaum Gate*, she has largely written her Catholicism out. It crops up again in the most recent novels, but it is only the ghost of itself, too much taken for granted to retain that offstage oracular presence so typical of the early fiction. A sense of personal identity

12. Emily Brontë, *Wuthering Heights*, 367.

from now on becomes less and less contingent on formal obser-
vance, more and more on the collaboration of the believer with the
promptings of the Spirit. This is not to say that the novelist sanc-
tions a policy of spiritual laissez-faire—the treatment of Hubert's
cult in *The Takeover* is proof enough of her impatience with such
attitudes—but it is to affirm that a fussy and formalistic religion has
become anathema to her. She has, to use a Lutheran term, become
an adiaphorist, and seems to imply that the Church can no longer
claim absolute obedience after the turmoil of Vatican II, simply
because it has begun to speak with many voices. One can assume
that the dark, secular *novelle* of the seventies derive, if not from a
crisis of faith, then at least from an impatience with conventional
notions of salvation, for a church torn apart is no longer able to
exert any stabilizing force upon the life of the individual.

While it is possible that humanists might welcome the muting of
the Catholic note in the novels that follow *The Mandelbaum Gate*, its
absence, like the absence of a dominant pedal that would give tension and counterthrust to an otherwise ordinary sequence of har-
monies, issues in mufflement and thinness. Before *The Public Image*,
Spark's Catholicism had provided a sounding board and resonator
for nuances that might otherwise have been sacrificed to a tempo
quite often too brisk for its own good. We have seen the author
compliment those of her novels which race, and race they certainly
do, even bulky ones like *The Mandelbaum Gate*. The rapid, disen-
gaged treatment of complex issues would invite charges of superficiality, were that treatment not steadied by the weight and solidity
of the doctrine it coasts over and guides itself by. Let us glance, for
example, at the coda of *Memento Mori*: "Miss Valvona went to her
rest. Many of the grannies followed her. Jean Taylor lingered for a
time, employing her pain to magnify the Lord, and meditating sometimes confidingly upon Death, the first of the four last things ever to
be remembered."[13] Here is that characteristic race, that quick, dispassionate disposal of narrative matter that Christopher Isherwood
in another context, describing a moment in Forster's *The Longest
Journey*, has called "tea-tabling." But, through the allusion to the
"Magnificat," and through the reference to the Four Last Things,
the prose trembles with deeper reverberations—we hear the cadences
of the Gospel according to St. Luke, and behind them the cadences
of the song of Hannah, and alongside those in turn the majestic
discourse of the Revelation of St. John. Musically responsive read-

13. Spark, *Memento Mori*, 246.

ers, moreover, have their experience of the text additionally enriched by memories of Bach and Pergolesi, and of Mozart, Berlioz, and Verdi. In this way the apparently superficial procedure, by clearing away "lateral" distraction in the form of circumstantial detail, has made possible a vertical penetration to the underpinning dogma, in much the same way as a good, which is to say a profound, epigram can use its limitation to imply a consciousness of what its pattern has forced it to forego stating. As the transcendent vision of the Rye enriches the scope of the novel it completes, so the transcendent vision humanizes the dangerously inhuman pace of the narrative in Memento Mori, and a good many other works besides.

If we turn to the final moment of The Public Image, which marks the start of the "exilic" phase, we at once become conscious of an impoverishment in timbre and concern. Here the author does not conceive the individual's destiny in heroic terms, as a conformation to the strenuous demands of faith. Annabel Christopher's vocation is, in contrast, self-constructed and minimal:

> Waiting for the order to board, she felt both free and unfree. The heavy weight of the bags was gone; she felt as if she was still, curiously, pregnant with the baby, but not pregnant in fact. She was pale as a shell. She did not wear her dark glasses. Nobody recognized her as she stood, having moved the baby to rest on her hip, conscious also of the baby in a sense weightlessly and perpetually within her, as an empty shell contains, by its very structure, the echo and harking image of former and former seas.[14]

This is Annabel Christopher disencumbered, disencumbered of the material possessions her former life as a film star has given her—suggested as an absence of baggage—and disencumbered of the falsehoods upon which that life has been based. Clearly the moment is vocational, and it seems to be based on the same sharp division of experience that underlies Nicholas's conversion in The Girls of Slender Means. Yet, for all that, its effect is feeble. The spare, elegant attenuation of the prose has to create its values from within itself: it has no allusive resource of Scripture and liturgy to enrich its slim lines. Given Spark's admiration of Proust (a writer who invariably inspires her to write), one can trace the shell image to his suggestion that if the cathedrals of France were turned into monuments, they would become little more than beautiful seashells, devoid of the life they

14. Spark, The Public Image, 192. Hereafter cited parenthetically in the text by page number.

were designed to hold. Proust envisages cathedrals as liturgically active spaces, not museums, and his image stresses a potential impoverishment. So too does Spark's, though it paradoxically presents its impoverishment as a virtue. Viewed *sub specie aeternitatis* (as it would have been in the earlier novels), Annabel's choice to renounce a specious for a real life would have seemed an obligation too obvious even for thought of any alternative. In *The Public Image*, on the other hand, viewed *sub specie mundi*, it takes on the quality of heroic anagnorisis. The mere litotes of refusing any longer to live a lie (and it is in any case a decision precipitated by blackmail) now does service as a decision to live the truth. The two are clearly not commensurate, and the fact that the realms of the expedient and the moral should collapse into each other measures the flaccid quality of the novels coming in the wake of *The Mandelbaum Gate*. One is tempted to quote Annabel against herself: "Good? What's good about not being bad?" (p. 175). This moral pallor escapes condemnation in the writer's applause of Annabel's unpainted face, the pallor of which is meant to register as "truth." And so the novel lodges finally on an image of vacuity, the oceanic compass of the shell's whisper amounting to nothing more than an acoustic illusion. The closed verbal rebound of "former and former" enacts that vacant echo, an echo resembling the meaningless circuit of Macbeth's "Tomorrow and tomorrow and tomorrow," though its "former" reverses it through a meaningless past instead of projecting it into a meaningless future.

An additional source of impoverishment in Spark's "dark" phase is its focus on the leisured rich. There is perhaps no *necessary* aesthetic disadvantage in her choice, for it is after all the milieu that Henry James chose more and more obsessively to document as his fiction matured. But in James there is always the tempering presence of New World morality and earnestness as it confronts a decadent Europe through the International Theme. Such a tempering presence was supplied by the Catholic dogma that obtrudes so doggedly into the otherwise casual world of the first phase of Spark's novels. Its absence is all the more to be lamented in a milieu of immense power, where people, made tinpot demigods by excessive wealth, have no external system to give them purpose and forge their own deviant rules to flatter the deviant courses of their lives. The listlessness of such works as *The Public Image* and its congeners can thus be traced to the fatally detached account of a valueless society. As Karl Malkoff has noted, the "decision to place Annabel, in all her shallowness, near the center of consciousness proves a formidable obstacle. Banality always threatens . . . ."[15] Almost all the novels between *The Public Image* and *Loitering with Intent*, peopled with trivial "jet-setting" figures, themselves become infected with that triviality.

If writers plan to satirize futility, they need sturdier moral equipment than graceful cynicism. Satire requires passion if it is to sustain its corrective power. A Juvenal consumed with *saeva indignatio* might have engendered some sort of momentum as he led us through Spark's internationalist valley of the shadow of death, but Spark is no Juvenal. Essentially Horatian in her light, dismissive procedures, she often flags at her task. At their worst, the books read like valueless trifling. Indeed, the erasure of the Catholic dimension, hitherto the guarantor of high seriousness, gives to some the flavor of blasphemous parody. The writer even goes so far as to invert her grand theme in *The Driver's Seat*, a novel about the extinction of identity in a vocation to death. Patrick Parrinder has described this upsetting effort as "a slap in the face for feminists and anti-rape campaigners" (p. 26), and so in a sense it is. But it is also a slap in the face for other humane values that have informed and braced the earlier fiction. Lise's quest is a suicidal one, and suicide in the catechetic framework thrown round, for example, *Memento Mori* is the sin of despair, the unforgivable sin against the Holy Ghost. Spark's cool, dissociated procedures allow the satire to function in only the thinnest of ways, and the norms of judgment and redress, so close to the surface in the first phase, have slipped out of sight.

In *Not to Disturb* and *The Hothouse by the East River*, the etiolation and languor persist. We are trapped in that stifling round of ennui and purposelessness that an excess of wealth secures. Vocation, if it exists at all, is vocation to a life of hedonism, to filling a leisure made empty by privilege. A narrative sleight of hand in the New York novel makes it clear that this very social condition is a species of purgatory, its characters in endless suspicion of each other in an unstable and vaporous setting that keeps revising and rewriting itself. But because the narrator has absented her values, or kept them in reserve, the novel drifts with the same suspended purpose as its characters'. It creates the sense, not so much of an epigram arching up out of the counterthrust of experience against judgment, as of a fantastical short story by Spark, blown up gaseously to fit a format it has not the density to sustain. In its tired anaphoric sentences is the world-weariness of the Absurd:

15. *Muriel Spark*, 46.

She remembers Kiel very well. She remembers what happened when
we were engaged during the war. She knows that Kiel was a double
agent and went to prison after the war. She heard that he died in
prison and now she's seen him in New York. But if one makes any
appeal to her sense of its significance she's not interested. She's away
and out of reach. She looks out of the window and I stand there like a
grocer who's come to demand payment of an overdue bill from, say,
Michelangelo while he's up on the scaffold of the Sistine Chapel,
painting the ceiling. She says, "Go and get a drink." That's what she
says, and I'm only a little figure far beneath her and her thoughts.[16]

Anaphora, stripped of the psalmic exaltation it conveys in Hebrew
poetry, becomes a stuck groove in the hands of the Absurdist. Here,
by way of comparison, is an extract from *Waiting for Godot*:

ESTRAGON: Our movements.
VLADIMIR: Our elevations.
ESTRAGON: Our relaxations.
VLADIMIR: Our elongations.
ESTRAGON: Our relaxations.
VLADIMIR: To warm us up.
ESTRAGON: To calm us down.[17]

This deadpan deployment of a figure usually connected with ela-
tion provides a cue for Spark's studied repetitions of "she." And so
too its *acervatio*, its rhetorical heapings-up, not in a spirit of generosity but of despair, occurs in a later speech of Annie's, where the
whole of life is reduced to a list of problems that parade their insol-
ubility: "We already have the youth problem, the racist problem, the
distribution problem, the political problem, the economic problem,
the crime problem, the matrimonial problem, the ecological problem, the divorce problem, the domiciliary problem, the consumer
problem, the birth-rate problem," etc. (p. 129). This is meant to
subvert the humanist's sense of social responsibility, but in fact it
gives the writer a heartless detachment from what *are* in fact problems, though the inclusion of mischievous nonproblems such as
those of the "domiciliary" and "physiopsychodymanics," like the
"elongations" that Beckett inserts into his catalog of exercises, would
want to contaminate the whole list.

Not to Disturb exemplifies, perhaps more than any other work of
the period in question, another failing that Spark's later secularity
brings to the fore. Ever since the Middle Ages, analogues have been

16. Spark, *The Hothouse by the East River*, 22. Hereafter cited parenthetically in
the text by page number.
17. Samuel Beckett, *Waiting for Godot*, 76.

set up between the poet and the Creator, an analogue inherent in the very term *maker*. With the advent of the novel and its omniscient narration, the parallel became more striking still. Until then God alone had had access to the inward thoughts of the creature, but novelists, with all their penetrative resources at their disposal, could now replicate that awareness vis-à-vis their own creations. When the writer is as encyclopedic and grave and profound as, say, George Eliot, any sense of manipulation is lost in the texture of circumstantiality. There is little of the "palpable design" Keats banished from his conception of the ideal poem. However, when a novel picks up speed and handles its material with dispatch, that design becomes more and more insistent. It is evident in the work of Beerbohm, of Saki, and of Evelyn Waugh, writers whose work to some extent resembles Spark's, and it is evident above all in her own. For as long as the novelist creates the sense of a Providence of which she is simply the mediator, the danger of patness is more or less avoided. When, say, in *The Bachelors*, Alice makes the outcome of Seton's trial a test of her belief in God and renounces that belief at the very moment that the arraignment of Seton is saving her from death at his hands, the plot registers as a subtle acknowledgment of pattern beneath a chaos of accidentalities. But as the tone of the novels darkens, and secularity edges out the firm doctrinal substrate of the first phase, the plotting becomes discomfittingly glib. The writer is a shade too obviously the *dea artifex*, trimming and cutting and disposing, or delegating these activities to her fictional surrogates, Lise in *The Driver's Seat* and Lister in *Not to Disturb*. Life has none of the spontaneity of choice, shows few unpredictable irruptions of grace, little earnest struggle with circumstance. In Switzerland, cradle of Calvinist predestination, plot has become a scenario, and it is "produced" to the last detail of a blueprint. As in *The Public Image*, the manipulation and devalued clichés of the media are the target of the satire, and, as there, the absence of invigorating *indignatio* makes for a minimal, frigid effect. What was projected in *The Bachelors* and *The Girls of Slender Means* as the inscrutable pattern of Providence has become the arbitrariness and flatness of a palpable design. The humility that came of delegating responsible judgment to the body of faith submerged in the narrative, and even occasionally protruding through it, has given way to the Promethean arrogance that mocks the omnipotence of Jove with its own mud figures. It is not for nothing that the author uses a relentless present tense for novels of this type. The present, after all, is the tense of recipes:

Having alerted the police and quiveringly recommended an ambulance with attendant doctors and nurses, Lister now telephones to the discreet and well-appointed flat in Geneva which he prudently maintains, and extends a welcome to the four journalists who have been waiting up all night for the call, playing poker meanwhile, with ash-trays piled high.

"Our four friends," Lister then instructs the household, "are to have first preference in anything you can say to them. They will, of course, have the scandal exclusives which Mr. Samuel and Mr. McGuire have prepared in the form of typescript, photographs and sound-recordings. The television, Associated Press and the local riff-raff are sure to question you wildly: answer likewise—say anything to them, just anything, but keep them happy. Isn't that right, Clovis?"[18]

The closest the novel comes to any sense of calling is the telephone call—one summoning the journalists to record the prearranged death. This is a fitting parable for the way in which this repulsive novella is put together. Providence is nothing more than an efficient schedule, and the puppeteering Lister is most decidedly antihumanist in the way he denies the possibility of choice in the predestinations of his scenario. What Parrinder has said of Spark in general, and has blamed on her Catholicism, is true above all of a work where Catholicism is nowhere to be found. Again I would argue that its absence results in a loss both of moral and aesthetic stature.

When Spark returns to that enlivening intersection of faith and art from which her first novel came to birth, the fiction at once becomes more spirited. *The Abbess of Crewe* is, as we have seen, the fruit of this fictional reacquaintance with the basis of her faith. There is a marked difference, however. The Church of Rome has undergone throughout the sixties the seismic transformation of Vatican II, and its self-divisions are in marked contrast to the *immutable* corpus of dogma whose very immutability once supplied artistic discipline and purpose. It seems to me that whereas Caroline Rose and Barbara Vaughan have had to submit themselves to "the destructive element," to fashion vocation from principles that cut against the velleities of human instinct, the abbess takes advantage of ecclesiastical anarchy to make her own rule. She is one of the leisured rich transposed into a convent, but little different in her obsessiveness from Lise, or from Lister in her manipulativeness. In *The Abbess of Crewe*, vocation is parodied by internal subversion rather than by the displacement we find in the secular *novelle*.

Thus while the dark period seems to have yielded to the easier,

18. Spark, *Not to Disturb*, 144.

mellowed mode of *The Abbess of Crewe* and *The Takeover*, trivializ-
ing cynicism still persists. If the convent novel is about the chaos
and laissez-faire of Vatican II, *The Takeover* suggests that Spark has
subsequently had to contend with a phenomenon even more trying
to herself—the arrival of Protestant Pentecostalism in the Church of
Rome. Although the prose is ostensibly tracking the thoughts of
Hubert here, the narrative has not shown him to glean any firsthand
experience of the Charismatics, and it is easy to detect authorial
distaste in its unguarded adjectives. The distaste, ironically enough,
is strong enough to energize the satire, to give it a body of feeling
that breaks out of the playfulness one finds in *The Abbess of Crewe*:
"It infuriated him to think of the crowds of charismatics in St.
Peter's Square, thumbing their guitars, swinging and singing their
frightful hymns while waiting for the Pope to come out on the
balcony" (pp. 206–7). In this babel of contending ecclesiastical demands, antinomianism must flourish. The regulating norms that
the author saw as the stabilizing and legitimating basis for satire
have been rendered relative by Jesuit and Charismatic alike. Vocation is not a penetration of the human soul by a divine summons,
but rather the endless reecho of a spirit trapped in solipsism.

In *Territorial Rights*, a later novel still, we find a "hero" discover-
ing himself through an antivocation to crime:

> But Giorgio had moved a sliding door which led into the spacious
> room which was to be Robert's hide-out. It was the moment he walked
> into it that the thought came to him, with a rush of pleasure: At last I'm
> home—I'm out of the trap.
>   It was the beginning of Robert's happy days, the fine fruition of his
> youth.[19]

It is true that the writer's irony is fixed by the glimpse of Samuel
Beckett in "happy days" and by the semantic wobble of fruition
("fruitful climax" and mere enjoyment—the noun derives from *fruor*),
but this inside-outing of divine and secular experience demeans the
idea of vocation. Traffic in the mock-heroic mode always flows both
ways. And even when she addresses central theological issues such
as the problem of pain in *The Only Problem*, Spark is too caught up
in her recent habits to give it any sort of resonance. Far greater
theologians than herself have confronted the topic and have had to
resign its complexities to the realm of faith. And nothing seems to
be achieved by having one of those international drifters (this one

19. Spark, *Territorial Rights*, 221.

the heir to a Canadian salmon fortune) annotate the Book of Job. Identifying the referent of "Leviathan," which is one of Harvey's concerns in this novel, hardly adds up to theodicy.

Later, in her reminiscential novels about life in the literary and publishing worlds of mid-century London, Spark is candid about the easing of her religious discipline. One senses, in the light of the passages below, that if she were to have rewritten *Robinson* at this stage of her career, she would have accorded much greater sympathy to the hero's position in relation to the Church, or, in reconceiving *The Comforters*, would have had Caroline Rose bunk the retreats that force her into contact with Georgina Hogg. The first manifesto comes from *Loitering with Intent*:

> I too was a Catholic believer but not that sort, not that sort at all. And if it was true, as Dottie always said, that I was taking terrible risks with my immortal soul, I would have been incapable of caution on those grounds. I had an art to practise and a life to live, and faith abounding; and I simply didn't have the time or the mentality for guilds and indulgences, fasts and feasts and observances. I've never held it right to create more difficulties of religion than already exist.[20]

Much the same sentiments are uttered by Mrs. Hawkins in *A Far Cry from Kensington*, who up to this point in the novel has religiously recited the Angelus at noon, braiding it silently into her telephone conversations:

> The more I heard of the Box, the more I was convinced, as I still am, that it was a lot of rubbish. But was it any more mad than my compulsive Hail Marys at twelve o'clock noon? I went on standing, looking at poor Wanda, in a dreadful state as she was. I decided then and there to give up those Hail Marys; my religion in fact went beyond those Hail Marys which had become merely a superstition to me.[21]

This is sudden and startling, and it relies on that startling suddenness to shock the reader into assent. Sober reflection, however, enables one to ask what the possible connection between the black box and the Angelus might be, and why the author can so electrically and swiftly posit the non sequitur. Having linked heterogeneous ideas together with a much more plausible violence in her early career, Spark here depends on her reader's not pausing too

20. Spark, *Loitering with Intent*, 130–31. Hereafter cited parenthetically in the text by page number.

21. Muriel Spark, *A Far Cry from Kensington*, 127. Hereafter cited parenthetically in the text by page number.

long in the race of the narrative to examine the claim, a claim as specious as the transition to Kensington at the end of the novel, surely one of the most irrelevant and meaningless in contemporary fiction:

> William was waiting for me at the car.
> "Did you settle the bill?" he said.
> I said, "Yes."
> It was a far cry from Kensington, a far cry. (p. 189)

Whatever the gnomic force of that conclusion (and I must confess that it eludes me), it is certainly a far cry from the Kensington of *The Bachelors,* and much the poorer for the distance of its cry. Vocation has become a self-issued fiat, not a collaborative response to the promptings of grace. This is not without its effect on the epigrammatic procedure that we have noted as an informing feature of the fiction, which thus forfeits the reassurance of a body of doctrine, solidly there, to be dipped into as occasion demands.

The Four Last Things, for example, which we have seen give such density and pathos to the dispatch with which age is otherwise handled in *Memento Mori,* cannot enter novels like *Loitering with Intent* and *A Far Cry from Kensington* with the same status of pre-formulated verities, to be invoked as a source of security, a guarantee of substance, a licence to the author for sweeping and airy capsulations of experience. Faith in the late novels becomes a process of selection, and process of its very nature cannot conduce to the finish of epigram. The technique of condensation and patterning is not discarded—far from it—but is applied less relentlessly and with a greater human warmth than the author allowed herself in her inglorious middle phase. The "free advice" that Mrs. Hawkins offers throughout *A Far Cry from Kensington* is perhaps symptomatic of the change. It is lived-through wisdom rather than the crisp, patterned formulations of epigram that sets the tone. The valedictory image of *Loitering with Intent* sums it up most cogently: "Some small boys were playing football, and the ball came flying straight towards me. I kicked it with a chance grace, which, if I had studied the affair hard, I never could have done" (p. 222). Even so, it is the novels of Spark's first phase, novels of "hard study" that most frequently manage "chance grace," grace which is not simply airy elegance, as here, but grace in the profounder sense, born in part of doctrinal confidence. For it is in these terms, not her later ones, that she most plausibly traces the connection between vocation and the proper flowering of the self.

In the context of Feuerbach's humanism, *Homo homini Deus*: humankind becomes the god of humankind. The program, which promises liberation, also contains in its formulation the circuit of self-entrapment: *homo homini*. All sense of the transcendent other has been abolished, and in its place is the reflected image of the self. There is also the hint of self-worship, of the self's creating itself in its own image, and finding that it is good. Whether or not one assents to the metaphysical framework that encloses the best of Muriel Spark's novels, there can be no doubting that it ensures against solipsism and vainglory, against being, as the Old Man of the Mountain says to Peer Gynt, "to thyself . . . enough."[22] These, the negative bequests of a humanism that came to birth as an assertion of human dignity, have quite as often inflated the littleness of humankind as they have realized the excellence of its potential. With premises very different from Spark's, David Ehrenfeld has traced a number of global woes to the humanistic vision: ". . . there are good and evil sides to humanism, and it is time to recognize the evil side for what it is and the damage it does."[23] Novels that warn us of "that evil side," no matter how disconcertingly and uncompromisingly unfashionable the tenets of the warning, are novels to cherish. The least way to honor them is to read them in the terms that they offer: imaginatively, at least, to agree that it is in the severe limitation of the self, not its infinite aggrandizement, that moral health is to be found.

22. Henrik Ibsen, *Peer Gynt*, 69.
23. *The Arrogance of Humanism*, 20.

Bibliography

Works by Muriel Spark

The Abbess of Crewe. London: Macmillan, 1974.
The Bachelors. London: Macmillan, 1960.
The Ballad of Peckham Rye. London: Macmillan, 1960.
Collected Stories I. London: Macmillan, 1967.
The Comforters. London: Macmillan, 1957.
Doctors of Philosophy. In *Novelists' Theatre.* Introduced by Eric Rhode. Harmondsworth: Penguin, 1966.
The Driver's Seat. London: Macmillan, 1970.
A Far Cry from Kensington. London: Constable, 1988.
The Girls of Slender Means. London: Macmillan, 1963.
The Hothouse by the East River. London: Macmillan, 1973.
Loitering with Intent. London: The Bodley Head, 1981.
The Mandelbaum Gate. London: Macmillan, 1965.
Memento Mori. London: Macmillan, 1959.
Not to Disturb. London: Macmillan, 1971.
The Only Problem. London: The Bodley Head, 1984.
The Prime of Miss Jean Brodie. London: Macmillan, 1961.
The Public Image. London: Macmillan, 1968.
Robinson. London: Macmillan, 1958.
The Stories of Muriel Spark. London: The Bodley Head, 1985.
The Takeover. London: Macmillan, 1976.
Territorial Rights. London: Macmillan, 1979.

Secondary Sources

Anon. *The Cloud of Unknowing.* Edited by James Walsh, S.J. New York, Ramsey, and Toronto: Paulist Press, 1981.
Arnold, Matthew. *Literature and Dogma: An Essay Towards a Better Apprehension of the Bible.* London: Smith, Elder, & Co., 1891.
Baldanza, Frank. "Muriel Spark and the Occult." *Wisconsin Studies in Contemporary Literature* 6 (1965): 190–203.

Beckett, Samuel. *Waiting for Godot.* London: Faber, 1965.

Bradbury, Malcolm. "Muriel Spark's Fingernails." *Critical Quarterly* 14 (1972): 241–50.

Brontë, Emily. *Wuthering Heights.* Edited by David Daiches. Harmondsworth: Penguin, 1965.

Casson, Allan. "Muriel Spark's *The Girls of Slender Means.*" *Critique: Studies in Modern Fiction* 7 (1965): 94–96.

Cavafy, C. P. *The Complete Poems of Cavafy.* Translated by Rae Dalven. London: The Hogarth Press, 1961.

Dante. *The Vision, or Hell, Purgatory, and Paradise of Dante Alighieri.* Translated by The Rev. Henry Francis Cary. London: Frederick Warne, [1844?].

Davison, Peter. "The Miracles of Muriel Spark." *Atlantic Monthly* 222 (1968): 139–42.

de Lubac, Henri, S.J. *The Drama of Atheist Humanism.* Translated by Edith M. Riley. 1950; rpt. Cleveland: The World Publishing Company, 1963.

de Rougemont, Denis. *Passion and Society.* Translated by Montgomery Belgion. London: Faber, 1956.

Dierickx, J. "A Devil Figure in a Contemporary Setting: Some Aspects of Muriel Spark's 'The Ballad of Peckham Rye.'" *Revue des Langues Vivantes* 33 (1967): 576–87.

Dobie, Ann B. "Muriel Spark's Definition of Reality." *Critique: Studies in Modern Fiction* 12 (1970): 20–27.

———. "The Prime of Miss Jean Brodie: Muriel Spark Bridges the Credibility Gap." *Arizona Quarterly* 25 (1969): 217–28.

Dobie, Ann B., and Wooton, Carl. "Spark and Waugh: Similarities by Coincidence." *Midwest Quarterly* 13 (1972): 423–34.

Dorenkamp, J. H. "Moral Vision in Muriel Spark's *The Prime of Miss Jean Brodie.*" *Renascence* 33 (1980): 3–9.

Drabble, Margaret. "*The Takeover.*" *New York Times Book Review,* 3 October 1976, 16–17.

Duff, J. W. *A Literary History of Rome in the Silver Age.* 1927; rpt. Westport, Conn.: Greenwood Press, 1964.

Ehrenfeld, David. *The Arrogance of Humanism.* New York: Oxford University Press, 1978.

Enright, D. J. "Public Doctrine and Private Judging." *New Statesman* 68 (1965): 563, 568.

Frankel, Sara. "An Interview with Muriel Spark." *Partisan Review* 54 (1987): 443–57.

Frazer, Sir James George. *The Golden Bough: A Study in Magic and Religion.* Abridged ed. 2 vols. London: Macmillan, 1957.

Gilbert, Sir W. S. *The Savoy Operas, Being the Complete Text of the Gilbert and Sullivan Operas as Originally Produced in the Years 1875–1896.* London: Macmillan, 1962.

Gillham, Ian. "Keeping It Short." *The Listener* 84 (1970): 411–13.

Greene, George. "*Du Côté de Chez Disaster:* The Novels of Muriel Spark." *Papers on Language and Literature* 16 (1981): 295–315.

Greene, Graham. *The Heart of the Matter.* London: William Heinemann, 1948.

Grosskurth, Phyllis. "The World of Muriel Spark: Spirits or Spooks?" *Tamarack Review* 39 (1966): 62–67.

Halio, Jay L. "Muriel Spark: The Novelist's Sense of Wonder." *British Novelists since 1900.* Edited by Jack I. Biles. New York: ASM Press, 1987.

Hammond, N. G. L., and Scullard, H. H., eds. *The Oxford Classical Dictionary.* Oxford: Clarendon Press, 1970.

Harrison, Bernard. "Muriel Spark and Jane Austen." In *The Modern English Novel: The Reader, the Writer and the Work,* edited by Gabriel Josipovici. London: Open Books, 1976.

Heawood, Geoffrey L. *The Humanist-Christian Frontier.* London: SPCK, 1969.

Holloway, John. "Narrative Structure and Text Structure: Isherwood's *A Meeting by the River* and Muriel Spark's *The Prime of Miss Jean Brodie.*" *Critical Inquiry* 1 (1975): 581–604.

Hosmer, Robert E. "The Book of Job: The Novel of Harvey." *Renascence* 39 (1987): 442–49.

Hoyt, Charles Alva. "Muriel Spark: The Surrealist Jane Austen." In *Contemporary British Novelists,* edited by Charles Shapiro. Carbondale and Edwardsville: Southern Illinois University Press, 1965.

Hynes, Joseph. *The Art of the Real: Muriel Spark's Novels.* London and Toronto: Associated University Presses, 1988.

Hynes, Samuel. "The Prime of Muriel Spark." *Commonweal* 75 (1962): 562–68.

Ibsen, Henrik. *Peer Gynt: A Dramatic Poem.* Translated with an Introduction by Peter Watts. Harmondsworth: Penguin, 1970.

Jacobsen, Josephine. "A Catholic Quartet." *Christian Scholar* 47 (1964): 139–54.

Joyce, James. *A Portrait of the Artist as a Young Man.* London: Jonathan Cape, 1964.

Kelleher, V. M. K. "The Religious Artistry of Muriel Spark." *Critical Review* 18 (1976): 79–92.

Kemp, Peter. *Muriel Spark.* London: Paul Elek, 1974.

Kermode, Frank. "Muriel Spark." In Continuities. London: Rout-
ledge and Kegan Paul, 1968.
———. "The House of Fiction: Interviews with Seven English Nov-
elists." Partisan Review 30 (1963): 61–82.
———. "The Prime of Miss Muriel Spark." New Statesman 66
(1963): 397–98.
———. "Sheerer Spark." The Listener 84 (1970): 425–26.
Keyser, Barbara. "Muriel Spark, Watergate, and the Mass Media."
Arizona Quarterly 32 (1976): 146–53.
———. "Muriel Spark's Gargoyles." Descant 20 (1975): 32–39.
———. "The Transfiguration of Edinburgh in The Prime of Miss
Jean Brodie." Studies in Scottish Literature 12 (1975): 181–89.
Kimball, Sue L. "Intentional Garble: Irony in the Communication of
Muriel Spark." West Virginia Philological Papers 33 (1987): 86–91.
Knight, Margaret. A Humanist Reader from Confucius to Bertrand
Russell. London: Barrie and Rockcliff, 1961.
Laffin, Gerry S. "Muriel Spark's Portrait of the Artist as a Young
Girl." Renascence 24 (1972): 213–23.
Little, Judy. Comedy and the Woman Writer: Woolf, Spark, and Femi-
nism. Lincoln: University of Nebraska Press, 1983.
Lodge, David. "The Uses and Abuses of Omniscience: Method and
Meaning in Muriel Spark's The Prime of Miss Jean Brodie." Criti-
cal Quarterly 12 (1970): 235–57.
McBrien, William. "Muriel Spark: The Novelist as Dandy." In
Twentieth-Century Women Novelists, edited by Thomas F. Staley.
London: Macmillan, 1982.
Malin, Irving. "The Deceptions of Muriel Spark." In The Vision
Obscured: Perceptions of Some Twentieth-Century Catholic Novel-
ists, edited by Melvin J. Friedman. New York: Fordham Univer-
sity Press, 1970.
Malkoff, Karl. Muriel Spark. New York: Columbia University Press,
1968.
Maritain, Jacques. True Humanism. Translated by M. R. Adamson.
London: Geoffrey Bles, 1938.
Marmion, The Right Reverend Columba. Christ, the Life of the Soul:
Spiritual Conferences. Translated by a Nun of Tyburn Convent.
London: Sands and Co., 1921.
Massie, Allan. Muriel Spark. Edinburgh: Ramsay Head, 1979.
Ohmann, Carol B. "Muriel Spark's Robinson." Critique: Studies in
Modern Fiction 8 (1965): 70–84.
Parrinder, Patrick. "Muriel Spark and Her Critics." Critical Quar-
terly 25 (1983): 23–31.

Paul, Anthony. "Muriel Spark and *The Prime of Miss Jean Brodie*." *Dutch Quarterly Review of Anglo-American Letters* 7 (1977): 170–83.

Potter, Nancy A. J. "Muriel Spark: Transformer of the Commonplace." *Renascence* 17 (1965): 115–20.

Price, Martin. "Believers: Some Recent Novels." *Yale Review* 63 (1972): 80–91.

———. "Reason and Its Alternatives: Some Recent Fiction." *Yale Review* 58 (1969): 464–74.

Ray, Philip E. "Jean Brodie and Edinburgh: Personality and Place in Murial [sic] Spark's *The Prime of Miss Jean Brodie*." *Studies in Scottish Literature* 13 (1978): 24–31.

Richmond, Velma Bourgeois. "The Darkening Vision of Muriel Spark." *Critique: Studies in Modern Fiction* 15 (1972): 71–85.

———. *Muriel Spark*. New York: Frederick Ungar Publishing Co., 1984.

Rochefoucauld, François, Duc de la. *Reflections; or Sentences and Moral Maxims*. London: Samson, Low, 1871.

Rowe, Margaret Moan. "Muriel Spark and the Angel of the Body." *Critique: Studies in Modern Fiction* 28 (1987): 167–76.

Sanders, Wilbur. *John Donne's Poetry*. Cambridge: Cambridge University Press, 1971.

Schneider, Harold. "A Writer in Her Prime: The Fiction of Muriel Spark." *Critique: Studies in Modern Fiction* 5 (1962): 28–45.

Schneider, Mary W. "The Double Life in Muriel Spark's *The Prime of Miss Jean Brodie*." *Midwest Quarterly* 18 (1977): 418–31.

Snow, Lotus. "Muriel Spark's Uses of Mythology." *Research Studies of Washington State University* 45 (1977): 38–44.

Spark, Muriel. "Edinburgh-born." *New Statesman* 65 (1962): 180.

———. "The Mystery of Job's Suffering: Jung's New Interpretation Examined." *Church of England Newspaper*, 15 April 1955, 7.

———. "The Religion of an Agnostic: A Sacramental View of the World in the Writings of Marcel Proust." *Church of England Newspaper*, 27 November 1953, 1.

———. "The Sermons of John Henry Newman." *Critic* (1964): 27–29.

Stanford, Derek. *Muriel Spark*. Fontwell: Centaur Press, 1963.

———. "The Work of Muriel Spark: An Essay on Her Fictional Method." *The Month* 28 (1962): 92–99.

Stubbs, Patricia. *Muriel Spark*. London: Longman, 1973.

Updike, John. "Creatures of the Air." *The New Yorker*, 30 September 1961, 161–67.

———. "Fresh from the Forties." *The New Yorker,* 8 June 1981, 148–56.

———. "Seeresses." *The New Yorker,* 29 November 1976, 164–74.

———. "Topnotch Witcheries." *The New Yorker,* 6 January 1975, 76–78.

Walker, Dorothea. *Muriel Spark.* Boston: Twayne, 1988.

Weatherby, W. J. "Muriel Spark: My Conversion." *Twentieth Century* 170 (1961): 58–63.

Welsford, Enid. *The Fool: His Social and Literary History.* London: Faber and Faber, 1935.

Whittaker, Ruth. *The Faith and Fiction of Muriel Spark.* London: Macmillan, 1982.

Wilce, Gillian. "Her Life in Fiction." *New Edinburgh Review* 55 (1981): 13–14.

Wildman, John Hazard. "Translated by Muriel Spark." In *Nine Essays in Modern Literature,* edited by Donald E. Stanford. Baton Rouge: Louisiana State University Press, 1965.

Index

Absurdism, 12, 18, 26, 78, 141, 149–50
Adiaphorism, 146
Alacoque, Saint Margaret Mary, 109
Albigensians, 101
Alexander VI, Pope, 96
Alighieri, Dante. *See* Dante
Anarchism, 45, 49
Andersen, Hans, 43
Anglicanism, 118
Antinomianism, 19, 91, 111, 153
Aristotle, 30
Arnold, Matthew, 137, 140
Auden, W. H., 47, 125, 133
Augustinianism, 24
Austen Jane: *Mansfield Park*, 18, 136

Bach, Johann Sebastian, 147
Bacon, Francis, 127
Baldwin, Monica, 104
Barrie, J. M., 38
Beaumarchais, Pierre-Augustin de: *Le Mariage de Figaro*, 86
Beckett, Samuel, 86, 139, 153; *Waiting for Godot*, 150
Beerbohm, Max, 151
Bergson, Henri, 9, 12, 44
Berkeley, Bishop George, 50, 99, 107
Berlioz, Hector, 147
Bernstein, Carl, 99
Bible, The: 2 Corinthians, 31; Ecclesiastes, 10, 45; Genesis, 95; Job, 10, 99, 154; Joel, 94; Matthew, 138; 1 Peter, 107,

110; Psalms, 80; Revelation, 71, 82, 146; 1 Thessalonians, 145
Blake, William, 46
Boileau, Nicolas, 100
Breton, André, 98
Brontë, Emily: *Wuthering Heights*, 145
Browning, Robert, 14, 72–73, 103, 136
Buñuel, Luis, 103
Byron, Lord George Gordon, 40

Calvinism, 151
Catholicism, 14ff., 135ff.
Catullus, 96
Cavafy, Constantine, 42
Chagall, Marc, 96
Cloud of Unknowing, The, 22, 27, 81
Coleridge, Samuel Taylor, 26; *The Ancient Mariner*, 55
Compton-Burnett, Ivy, 9
Covenanters, 101
Cranmer, Thomas, 23

Dali, Salvador, 98, 103
Dante: *The Divine Comedy*, 10, 75, 86, 137
de Caussade, Jean-Pierre, 80
Defoe, Daniel, 144
de Quincey, Thomas, 86
Dickens, Charles: *A Christmas Carol*, 124; *Little Dorritt*, 18
Disney, Walt, 93, 108
Donne, John, 14
Dostoyevsky, Fyodor, 139

163